The
BIG
BUCKET
LIST
BOOK

133 EXPERIENCES
OF A LIFETIME

GIN SANDER

Published by Sourcebooks, Inc.
P.O. Box 4410, Naperville, Illinois 60567-4410
(630) 961-3900
Fax: (630) 961-2168
www.sourcebooks.com

Library of Congress Cataloging-in-Publication data is on file with the publisher.

Printed and bound in the United States of America.

VP 10 9 8 7 6 5 4 3 2 1

For Bryan, who has led a most remarkable life and
continues to inspire me to head out in search of adventure,
and for David, who happily accompanies me as I do.

·········· ✳ ··········

CONTENTS

THRILL YOUR TASTE BUDS: FOOD AND WINE

EXPERIENCES   23

MAKE YOUR MARK: IRRESISTIBLY FUN DIY ACTIVITIES

AND SKILLS   35

GIVING BACK: MAKE YOUR MARK   **97**

.... * ....

INTRODUCTION

Are you at the point in life where you're looking for new ideas and adventures? Feeling in a rut, or just wanting to make sure you're enjoying your life to the fullest? You have come to the right place! We live in exciting times. Opportunity for personal growth and lasting adventure surrounds us if we dedicate ourselves to looking out for it. But in our busy, overworked, and distracted world, it can be easy to let those possibilities slip by. Every day I try to keep an open attitude in the hope it will steer me toward taking chances, stretching for goals, and continuing to move forward in life to experience as much as I can, as fully as I can.

Does that sound like a mantra for living that you'd like to embrace? Make it your own from now on with this book. In the pages to come I offer ideas for anyone at any point in his or her life—starting out, midway through a career, or winding down workwise—who wants to add a challenge, perhaps a touch of glamour, and a solid sense of satisfaction, enjoyment, and accomplishment to their pursuit of a well-lived life. This list includes unique travel destinations, a great many personal challenges, and more than a few unusual pastimes, and will amuse and delight readers with a host of new ideas. So let's get started.

THE WELL-LIVED LIFE?
DEFINE YOUR TERMS...

You might be wondering, "A well-lived life, according to *whom*?" No one wants to be told what to do, where to go, or how to think, of course. And that's not what this book aims to do. Rather, its goal is to inspire you to pursue exciting new experiences you've always dreamed of (and some you may have never imagined), whether those experiences are halfway across the world or right in your own backyard. Also, don't use this list as a reason to feel inadequate about what you've done in your life thus far. The world gives us plenty of chances to feel that way every day (and if you have children, I'm sure you've noticed that they will happily point your inadequacies out as well).

Instead, imagine you and I are having drinks in a wine bar, the soft afternoon light filtering in from the street while we enjoy a glass or two and swap ideas on things we'd like to accomplish before heading to that wine bar in the sky. You suddenly realize, why couldn't I finally try that hobby I've always been meaning to pick up? Or why couldn't I go on that trip I've dreamed of? Or maybe, in the course of the conversation, you even think of things you want to try that had never occurred to you.

That's what I did, of course. Had countless glasses and hours of conversation with well-traveled and accomplished people, listening to their goals and dreams, mentally adding the things that appealed to me to my own list. You'll hear from many of them in this book. Their perspectives and recounting of their experiences and ideas were enough to make me want to cut the conversation short and get going!

One friend told me he wanted to "die with his boots on."

"But Bryan," I pointed out, "you don't wear cowboy boots. You wear velvet slippers."

Yes he did, he admitted, in fact he had thirty pairs of custom-made slippers from a shoemaker in Venice. "Must go to Venice for velvet slippers," I thought to myself, smiling and sipping gin as he spoke. Simply must.

So what exactly do I mean by a "well-lived life"? Do I think we need to earn our spot on the planet and make full use of our talents, imaginations, and drives? No. Here is what a well-lived life means to me:

- That you have showered love and affection on those around you and received it in return.

- That the world is a better place because of your energy, generosity, creativity, and efforts.

- That you had the chance to get out in the world and poke around, not just to observe, but to fully engage with other people in other places.

- That you had a hand in creating something, somewhere that will outlive you.

In other words, I believe that to pursue a well-lived life you need to get out there and make something happen. Participate in life, rather than observe or drown in the dreaded feeling that it's just passing you by. But it's more than just putting another notch in your belt. Much was made of President Obama's ten-minute stop at Stonehenge during a state visit to England. "Knocked that off my bucket list," he said, climbing back into his motorcade and heading off to the next meeting. Is that all there is to some bucket lists, to merely view something of interest while making a mental check next to that item? There's something quite sad about that.

This book is designed to get you engaged in your life so that you fully experience it on all levels. Planning a trip to Paris? Great. Why not also plan to become a *part* of Paris? To have a business in Paris, to learn a skill in Paris, to rehab a house in Paris, to model clothes in Paris, to paint in Paris, to run a marathon in Paris, to make wine in Paris, to have your hair done in Paris… Are you getting the idea here?

Of course you no doubt already have a hundred ideas about the things you'd like to do in your life. You may have been keeping a list for years now. I hope that this book will help you find many interesting ways to add to the list of the things you've longed to do at some point in your life or figure out how you can turn your own bucket-list wishes into realities. Think of this book and the ideas inside as an extra bit of frosting that you have swiped off the edge of life's cake.

You'll find all kinds of bucket list ideas in this book—there are travel ideas, food-related ideas, sporty ideas—but I've also included creative challenges, lofty goals, and extravagant desires. What do I mean by those terms?

♦ Creative Challenges are things you can make, items of permanence, ideas that will stretch your talents and abilities and perhaps help you develop some new ones.

♦ Lofty Goals are just that—lofty as in way above our heads—so why not reach up and try? Save the world. Invent a better mousetrap. Write the great American novel. Leave something behind. Create something of permanence. Visit the over-the-top places you dream of, and enjoy the unique things you want to do once you get there.

• Extravagant Desires? Okay, let's just say it…these are things you'd like to own. To have in your life on a daily basis. Like the custom-made velvet slippers that my friend Bryan wears. Do you have to pay for your desires? You might. But there are creative ways to bring what you want into your life for less, so those are also included.

What are your creative challenges? Lofty goals? Extravagant desires? You will have to decide for yourself. We want you to consider all of these ideas, not just the ones that you know will appeal to who you are right now. Because who you are right now might change in the future…and one of these ideas might bring about that change.

CAN I AFFORD MY BUCKET LIST?

Daydreaming is free. Acting on your dreams can sometimes be quite costly. Of course, we would all love to have lives of financial ease and good fortune, where our wildest dreams are well within our means. But what if that isn't the case? Are there ways to make your dreams come true on a budget? What about on a shoestring? What about for free? Depending on what your dream entails, sure. Here are a few methods to bootstrap that bucket list:

- **Ask Your Friends to Join**—Traveling with a group is almost always cheaper than going alone. Being part of a group puts you in a position to bargain for a better deal. And if what you want is costly—a week in a castle or a month on a sailboat—getting a group together to split the cost might bring it all into reach. So share your dream any chance you get and look for those like-minded folks whose eyes light up when you describe it.

- **Start a Special Account**—A dedicated savings account earmarked for your dream trip or purchase can be a great incentive. Resolve to put in every stray bit of cash you come across—the two hundred you brought in from your garage sale, the twenty bucks you got returning aluminum cans, or the money you made selling your daughter's old textbooks on eBay.

- **Try to Get Comped**—Yes, in some circumstances travel writers get parts of their trips comped. And as a consequence, hordes of hopeful folks have declared themselves "writers." Travel writers for major magazines and papers don't actually accept free travel. That's against company policy. However, plenty of writers for small sites and publications do. You will need to get an assignment first, to pitch your article idea to an editor and get it approved, before you can truthfully tell a hotel that you are working on a story.

- **Work for It**—Big cruise lines always have speakers onboard. Are you a public speaker with a niche that fits the theme or destination of a cruise? Cruise lines also sometimes employ men to dance with the single women on board… Just a thought for the retired man with a talent for the dance floor.

GoFundMe has thousands of active campaigns from hopeful travelers with head-lines like "Female World Trip on Motorcycle." She'd raised $6,683 from eighty-eight donors when I checked. "Will Schmidt's Canada to Mexico Paddle" had raised $8,530 toward his goal from seventy-nine donors, and "Battleborn Pacific Challenge," a team of guys who rowed from San Francisco to Hawaii, raised more than £16,000, or about $24,000!

◆ **Crowdsource**—Websites like Kickstarter and GoFundMe make it possible to ask friends and strangers to put money into your dreams. Kickstarter might fund your bucket list dream of producing a small film or opening a vegan sandwich shop. GoFundMe leans more toward asking for contributions to travel. But do tread carefully. You don't want to lose friends over this.

◆ **Volunteer**—If your money is low and your hopes are high, perhaps volunteering at your dream destination is a possibility. But not every place will allow volunteers free access. Burning Man, for instance, welcomes volunteer help during the year and during the event itself, but warns that helping doesn't lead to free admission. So keep that in mind as you do your research.

ASK, AND YE JUST MIGHT RECEIVE

Why do some people lead such interesting lives and have such amazing experiences, while others just lead sort of bland and humdrum lives? Could be that the people in the first group have learned the art of the ask. It seems like such a simple thing, really, but it can be quite intimidating to think about. At a famed restaurant that everyone is talking about, why not ask the waiter if you can go back into the kitchen and meet the chef? The answer may be no, and there is no shame in that. But if the answer is yes, think of the extraordinary opportunity that just fell into your lap! A behind-the-scenes look at the world of an artist.

So think about it…who do you want to meet? Go ahead and try to make it happen. Make blind phone calls, send out inquiring letters and emails, see if you can get in touch with someone you find fascinating. What do you want to know? Never be afraid to call on experts or skilled amateurs. They love to talk about their passions. Where do you want to go? Always ask for help in getting behind the scenes. What is behind that door marked Off Limits anyway? Ask the guide and they just might be in the mood to show you. Take charge of building your own interesting life by speaking up and asking for something unusual.

Okay. Ready to work on your bucket list? Let's get started at amping up your life of adventure! Take a look at these ideas and see how many spark your fancy. And most of all, have fun.

.... ✳ ....

GALAS, PARTIES, AND GET-TOGETHERS:

Marvelous Ways to Mix, Mingle, and Meet New Friends

Opening Night

Longing for an evening of all-out glamour, with men in black tie and women in glittering, long dresses? Why not attend the opening night of an orchestra or opera company?

To be clear, this is not an inexpensive undertaking in most places. For example, the least expensive ticket to the New York Philharmonic's most recent opening-night gala was $1,500 for a preconcert reception, the concert itself, and a postconcert dinner. The San Francisco Symphony the same year had a $170 opening-night gala ticket that included the chance to enter the music hall on a red carpet, see a concert that included Bonnie Raitt singing with the orchestra, and then attend a late-night after-party in the street outside with dancing, desserts, and the sense that you were one of the VIPs.

Are these events packed with serious lovers of opera and symphonic music? No, the organizers of these high-priced fetes understand that many attendees just like to get dressed up and attend a fun evening of entertainment and music, so the programming is mostly lighter fare. Sometimes opening nights feature interesting new works that the company has commissioned. New York City Ballet likes to pair new works with new costumes by big-name designers for an extra bit of oomph on opening night. So take a look at what your area's orchestra offers, and shake the dust off your best tux or gown.

Create Your Own Club!

Feeling excluded by some social group? Wishing you had a close group of like-minded friends with similar interests? Recently moved to a new area and longing to meet new people? There's no time like the present to form your own social club. You could cast your net wide and form a group in your area to hike together or taste wine or discuss current events. Or you could cast a very narrow net, forming a group of people your own age with the same educational background and specific point of view as you. Sounds like many other clubs out there, doesn't it? Ah, but this time you get to name it!

For example, longtime journalist Judith Horstman and a few other like-minded writers had plenty of writing groups to belong to, but wanted a purely social club with their fellow scribes. "Writers Who Wine" was born to meet their need to hang out with other writers and not feel the need to compete. Starting from just a handful of people, the Facebook group now has more than four hundred members and hosts events in several western cities.

Is there much administrative headache involved in starting a club? Not if you don't want there to be. "It took ten minutes to form the club on Facebook, and we send out a group message to members once a month announcing which bar we will be meeting in," Judith says. "If no one shows up to the 'meeting,' it isn't a problem. At least we have some nice wine to drink."

So how can you find folks to join up with? How do you get the word out about the kind of social club you wish to create? Simple. Type this into your browser—www.meetup.com. Find the icon that says "Start a Meetup Group." Click on it. Follow the instructions. There, how simple is that?

RESOURCES

www.meetup.com

Go behind the Scenes on Broadway, at the Opera, or Anywhere

Ever listen jealously to a friend's long tale about the time they got to go backstage at a Broadway show, or were ushered into the inner sanctum of a museum, historic house, or national monument? How'd they pull that one off, anyway? Chances are they were "friends" of the organization.

This may seem pretentious or like an unfair hurdle, but it's not necessarily. The key here is to join. Donate. Volunteer. If you are willing to give your time and your money, private worlds will open up to you, giving you the chance to live your dreams by going behind the scenes at one of the places you love. This doesn't have to cost pots of money, mind you. Even joining at the lowest level of a "friends of" organization may entitle you to special treatment when you visit. Shorter lines and secret entrances to some museums; discounts in the gift shop, to be sure. Or how does this sound? Friends of the High Line, a group that supports the inner-city park in New York City, gives a specially designed Coach bag to those who support at the very highest level! At some places, all you have to do is donate your time to get special backstage access and privileges. Volunteers for the Chicago Architecture Foundation, for instance, get free membership, a gift shop discount, and opportunities for continuing education.

As you begin to plan a long-dreamed-of visit to a special site, go to the website and see if a supporters group is listed. If so, what special benefits will you get? A private tour at a particular level? Invitations to special receptions and galas? If this is something on your bucket list, even joining at a higher level for just one year might give you the chance to live your dream.

RESOURCES

www.thehighline.org/volunteers/

www.architecture.org

Host Your Own Literary Salon

No, I don't mean open a hair salon with lots of books or magazines for your customers to read. This is a salon strictly in the literary sense, like those found in Paris and London in centuries past, where attendees come together for stimulating conversation about the events of the day.

The most famous literary salons were hosted by women, so what an honor for us to be able to continue the tradition of helping to spread knowledge and intellectual curiosity. How can you create your own salon? Simple. Invite the most interesting people you know, even some you may only know in passing, to gather at your place. Email and social media make it easy to be bold in reaching out to people you may only be vaguely acquainted with but want to get to know better. A beautifully handwritten invitation (or a nice online invitation from a website like PaperlessPost.com or Evite.com) can also go a long way toward convincing an interesting someone on the edge of your social circle to take a chance on coming to your event.

Sunday afternoons are particularly good times for these, as they provide a pleasant and relaxing way to wind down the weekend with smart talk. Set out some good wine, good food, or small bites, and circulate among your guests. You might want to announce a theme in advance, perhaps a topic drawn from the day's headlines to spark discussion and the flow of ideas or thoughts. Or you might announce a challenge, "What can we do to save the planet?" or "Does anyone have any useful ideas on how to tame traffic downtown?"

Revolutions grew out of some salons, as did great works of art and literature. Who knows what your efforts might produce!

RESOURCES

Saturday Salon: Bringing Conversation and Community Back Into Our Lives (Valerie Davisson, Vaughn House, 2012)

Mr. Hearst Will See You Now

Is there a more iconic architectural fantasy of the American dream than Hearst Castle along the central California coast? Not only does it conjure up the image of its wealthy and eccentric owner, who shipped castles and monasteries back from Europe in crates to be reassembled inside his house, but it also comes with a healthy dose of Hollywood glamour. It was the place to see and be seen for decades in the early days of the movie business. Everyone came to stay for the weekend, arriving by train or boat.

The castle has long been open to the public for tours. But if you open your checkbook wide enough, you can also put on your finest holiday gear and attend the occasional black tie Holiday Feast. Held in the Refectory Dining Hall of Casa Grande, the main house, the atmosphere is one of regal elegance. You can live out your dream of being William Randolph Hearst and his lady love, Marion Davies. After dinner and dessert, the guests retire to Hearst's private movie theater to view a vintage film.

Attending a gala dinner at Hearst Castle is not an inexpensive undertaking. Recent ticket prices for the holiday event were $1,000 per person for members of Friends of Hearst Castle and $1,250 for non-members. The event sells out quickly and is not held every year. For information, call the office of the FHC at 805-927-2138.

RESOURCES

www.friendsofhearstcastle.com

Join the Explorers Club

Clubs. We mentioned them often. Why? Because…well, they're so darned clubby. And if you can get in the door, you must be clubby too. One of the coolest clubs in the world is the century old Explorers Club. "World's Largest Gathering of Explorers Coming to New York" was the recent information on their annual dinner, the world's largest gathering of pioneers in space exploration, on land, and in the oceans. Doesn't that sound like a room you'd like to be in? Alas, you really do have to be an explorer on a very high level to be a member, but you could be an associate member.

My friend Bob (who will otherwise go nameless in this story for reasons that will be quite clear) is quite the raconteur and loves to tell the story about his one visit to the Explorers Club during a private party. Among the guests was George Plimpton. "Where's the gin?" Plimpton asked loudly. When he learned there wasn't any, he immediately put a plan into action. Bob described their raid on a locked liquor cabinet in the club with great pride. Seems Bob was never invited again to an event at the club. Nevertheless, he did get a great cocktail-party story out of it.

As their website points out, "Becoming an associate of the Explorers Club can provide a steppingstone to eventual full membership in the club. By attending events, meeting club members, and learning more about the demanding world of exploration, associates may, on their own initiative, take an opportunity to join an expedition and pursue meaningful field research which would lead to greater qualifications toward possible membership status."

Now that sounds cool. And the clubhouse, in a town house on East Seventieth Street, is exactly what you'd think an Explorers Club would look like. Filled with animal trophies, leather-bound books, and overstuffed chairs.

The club also has public lectures regularly, so by attending one, you could come into contact with a full-fledged member who could then nominate you for associate member status. Check the events section of the website.

RESOURCES

www.explorers.org

Find Your Congregation or Community

While not everyone wants to go to church or embraces the idea of religion, as we age, we all feel the need for community. And church does give that to its congregants. So where can you go for community if you don't want to or can't go to church? That is the question Pippa Evans and Sanderson Jones had back in 2013, and they founded the Sunday Assembly movement as a result.

"Live better. Help often. Wonder more." These three beliefs are at the core of the group they founded in England. In just a few years, the group has grown to more than thirty chapters around the world. If there isn't already a Sunday Assembly gathering near you, you can found one yourself. See the "Start Your Own Assembly" section of their website.

RESOURCES

www.sundayassembly.com

Throw an Annual Theme Party

Do you read the social news with envy? Look at the glossy photos in *Vanity Fair* of the annual Oscar parties and sigh? You somehow pictured a more glamorous life as an adult, didn't you? So, what are you waiting for? Choose an over-the-top theme and get to work. "You know Susan? She has that Labor Day party every year up at the lake. Bob and Kim? They do that big Oscar party in town and then in the spring the wild game barbeque out at their ranch." Want to be mentioned in the same breath as well-known hosts and hostesses? Find an event or holiday that no one else in your circle is handling and put out the word. Step up and be the place to be for New Year's Day brunch or a Valentine's Day cocktail party. Perhaps a Flag Day extravaganza? You get to choose the theme, announce the dress code, and decide location and decor. Best of all, you only have to serve food and drinks that you enjoy.

Own a Hot Auction Item

Ever notice those announcements in the press about the impending auction of some famous person's possessions? For example, Sotheby's and the frenzy surrounding Jackie Kennedy Onassis's belongings in the late 1990s. Or the auction for the jewels of the Duchess of Windsor in Paris in the 1980s. The gardening tools of Bunny Mellon. Or the scotch decanters and cigarette holders of John Perona, the gentleman who owned the famed New York bar El Morocco, auctioned off in 2014, decades after he died.

Why buy from these auctions? Because it can be really fun to own things with an interesting provenance. You could own a piece of history! They give you something to talk about during dull moments at the table and connect you in a small way to the life of someone you admire.

Devoted collectors attend meetings and belong to clubs and organizations. They read up on their topic, they do original research, and they exchange information with each other. It is a community. Retired judge David Meeker is a world-class collector of all things Hemingway, not just manuscripts but photographs, letters, and other kinds of memorabilia. "It has been a major focus of my life," he says. "And I've met fascinating people as a result."

Being a fan of Hemingway's writing and of course totally dazzled by his lifestyle, I joined the Hemingway Society. Most of the other members seemed to be college professors who specialized in Hemingway's life and career, which it is safe to say is not my own background. But what the heck, I thought. And as a result of a small item I noticed in the society newsletter, just a few short months later I found myself organizing three different exhibits of little-seen pictures of Hemingway in Venice. Have I ever joined a literary society before? Nope. Had I ever organized a photo exhibit before? Nope. But now I have done both!

Stay current on what's being offered in upcoming auctions by signing up for the newsletters of Doyle's, Sotheby's, Christie's, and Heritage Auctions. Fun as it is to attend an auction in person, most major houses now let you view and bid on the goods online, once you are registered with them.

RESOURCES

www.doylenewyork.com

www.sothebys.com

www.christies.com

www.HA.com

Enjoy a Polo Match in the Summer Sun

You've worn clothing for the past few decades with that little emblem embroidered on it, the man on horseback with a polo mallet stretched over his head. Have you ever been to an actual polo match though? Walked out during the break in play to help stomp down the deep divots made from thundering hooves and swinging mallets? Sipped a summer drink while wearing a large hat and gazing at two teams fighting it out on horseback? It's really quite lovely.

Much of worldwide polo is played at rather posh and exclusive private clubs, inside the tightly guarded world of the very rich. Public events do get played for charities though, and watching the sport can truly be a once-in-a-lifetime experience. Cinnamon Vann attended a polo match for the first time and commented, "Oh yes, it should definitely be on anyone's bucket list. I loved the part where we went out, champagne glass in hand, to stomp down the ground for the second half."

You can stroll in the midst of splendor and supermodels at the events organized by the St. Regis hotel chain's polo efforts. (Check out their website for current information.) They are the sponsor of a large yearly event in the Hamptons and have recently begun one on the West Coast in the Sonoma wine country.

And if you are at a point in your life where you might want to climb astride and swing a mallet, there are camps that will teach you. Destination Polo is one that can take you even if, as their website says, you "just rode when I was a kid." In the summer months they are in the Virginia hunt country near Washington, DC. In the winter the operation moves to Wellington, Florida.

RESOURCES

www.stregispolo.com

www.destinationpolo.com

Share Your Birthday with Someone Famous

August 6 is Andy Warhol's birthday. Is it by chance your birthday too? March 14 is Einstein's birthday. October 16 is Oscar Wilde's. We all share a birth date with someone famous or noteworthy, so look up your birth date and see who you share with. Once you know, what can you do with the info? Throw a party, of course.

Year after year you've had a birthday party. Isn't it time you gave yourself, your friends, and your family a chance to celebrate in a different way? Instead of sending out invitations to a party for yourself, throw a party for your birthday twin instead.

"I really do send out invitations to Oscar Wilde's birthday party," says Julia Berenson. "October 16. Every year I announce how old he would be, and oh, by the way, it is my birthday too. He throws a much more interesting party than I do, trust me. Once I started this tradition, it really took on a life of its own. My friends go all out with costumes and party favors."

Get to work on figuring out how to celebrate your birthday "twin" at the next opportunity. If you don't already know what luminary you are connected to by birth, research it now.

RESOURCES

www.famousbirthdays.com

Be a Delegate at a National Convention

Those big party conventions look pretty exciting on television, don't they? Thousands of people all dressed in kooky red, white, and blue outfits—and the hats! Who wouldn't want to wear one of those outrageous, over-the-top hats? Oh yes, and then there is electing your party's presidential candidate, which is actually the point of it all.

Why not be a delegate to your party's national convention at least once? Each party in each state has its own process for electing or selecting delegates, so your best source of information is your political party's state headquarters website.

Step one, of course, would be to be very active in your local party organization. You will quickly learn the insider perspective on becoming a delegate. If you don't end up at the national convention, the state party conventions can be equally inspiring. And maybe you can wear a funny hat there too. If you aren't chosen to attend as a delegate, there is always a need for volunteers, so you can raise your hand for that as a way to have the same experience.

"Go to the edge of the cliff and jump off.
Build your wings on the way down."
—RAY BRADBURY

Check Out Classic and Vintage Car Shows

Every August the most beautiful cars in the world are gathered on a golf course lawn next to the Pacific Ocean. The Pebble Beach Concours d'Elegance is famed for the amazing automobiles on display. Gleaming, well-preserved, and very, very valuable.

If you are a fan of classic cars but owning a Concours-level car is not on your bucket list, a trip to a vintage show weekend may be the best way to soak up the beauty. For more than twenty years, the exclusive Ocean Reef Club in Key Largo, Florida, has opened its doors to nonmembers once a year for its Vintage Weekend. Held the first weekend in December, the event is a four-day celebration of antique and classic cars, planes, and yachts. Find information at www.oceanreef.com.

One of the most perfect moments in my life occurred in August 1995. My young son Julian was in an English pram, napping sweetly as I pushed him along the closely cropped lawn at Pebble Beach, strolling from car to car. I had a baby, a fancy pram, and the smug knowledge that at home in the garage I had a vintage 1973 Mercedes 280 SEL with a monster 4.5 liter engine. The angels smiled on me that day. But that perfect moment passed all too quickly. The boy grew up, and the car actually exploded in a fire one day! It took years before I could forget the sight of a flaming Mercedes and come around to the idea of having an old car again. But now that I do have one again, every so often I think, hey, maybe this right-hand-drive 1966 Jaguar 3.4S that I bought last year off someone's front lawn could be restored to that Concours level. Maybe…

Lower key are vintage events at which "it is not so much about the cars as the life lived around them," enthusiast JT Long says. "The owners build a community around showing cars. They sit next to their old car in a folding chair, spectators come up, and they get to tell the story of how they brought their baby home from the hospital in that car, or they had their first date with their wife." JT and her partner, Bill Sessa, run a website, benchseatchronicles.com, for those kinds of stories.

Get Your Own Crown and Royal Entourage

Remember the old television show *Queen for a Day*? Back in the 1960s, housewives competed with sob stories to see which of them most deserved not only to be crowned "queen" but also to get new appliances that would make their lives of household drudgery a bit easier. Imagine that feeling of wearing a crown…even if you know it is a temporary thing. You might stand up a bit straighter, hold in your tummy, and throw back your shoulders. Swedish brides always wear crowns, a tradition that continues to this day.

I've said this already, but it can't be reiterated enough. To really live a fulfilling life, don't keep your dreams and goals to yourself. Share them out loud. Often. That will take you one step closer to achieving them. And don't be surprised if some of the folks you share with want to join you in your dream. Get a team together and go for it!

How can you get this feeling in real life? Tracie Stafford has had it several times. As an adult she began entering beauty competitions at a moment in her life when she needed a new challenge. "Win or lose, it is the journey that shapes your life," she says. "Pageantry not only helped me see all of myself as one amazing package, but also taught me to stand in my power regardless of the competition. It was an opportunity to showcase myself, my life, and my accomplishments. There is no better feeling than knowing how far you have come, I'm grateful that I had the courage to check this lifelong dream off of my bucket list." Where did her courage take her? She has been a first, second, and third runner-up many times, but also has been Mrs. California United States and Mrs. California Globe.

If you aren't up to the idea of a beauty competition, why not create your own royal entourage? March in a parade with friends, all bedecked in rhinestones and tiaras. Or start a club that includes a crowning element. Texas beauty shop owner Kathy Murphy created a book club that now has a national reputation—the Pulpwood Queens—to live a tiara-wearing, book-sharing life.

RESOURCES

www.tiaratown.com

www.tiarasandcrowns.com

www.beautyandthebook.com

·········· ✻ ··········

THRILL YOUR TASTE BUDS:
Food and Wine Experiences

Spend an Evening in a Wine Cave

Close your eyes and imagine the scene. You are below the earth—far below the earth, in some cases—in a cave with curved walls and surrounded by aging wines in oak barrels. The air is the perfect temperature, candlelight flickers on the walls, and a large table is set with gleaming crystal glasses and china plates. Dinner should be like this every night…

"It is an experience of a lifetime," sommelier Roxanne Langer says of dinner in a wine cave. "You are getting a winery chef who knows the wines perfectly and can pair the food accordingly. The romantic setting, the food and wine pairing—it is an incomparable evening for any food and wine lover."

Can you just show up at a wine cave with a picnic basket and sit down? No. These experiences need to be closely coordinated with the winery staff. Although many wineries with caves are open to corporate events, hosting your own private dinner party with friends might entail a little convincing. Joining the winery's club and receiving monthly shipments of wine often includes access to events in the wine caves and could get you closer to using it yourself.

Ladera, in California's Napa wine country, allows members of their Premiere Crew Wine Club to host private dinners in the wine caves. Based around a stunning stone building built in the 1880s, Ladera's wine cave dinners are held on an enormous redwood table made from the original floors and lit by candles made by the owners' daughter.

Food and wine are not the only delights you might find in a wine cave. Music is also found belowground.

Roxanne has worked in the Napa Valley for decades and knows which caves are best suited for your bucket list experience. You can ask her for friendly advice and help at roxanne@wine-fundamentals.com.

> **RESOURCES**
> www.laderavineyards.com
> www.musicinthevineyards.com

Take a Turn as an Apprentice Farmer

For decades, farm kids were desperate to escape the country life and head to the city to do anything other than farm. The reverse is now true, with many city dwellers now dreaming of a life on the farm. Is this your dream too? In the past, the only way to learn to farm was to grow up on one. But now you can actually live and work at a farm school.

The Essex Farm in New York offers the Essex Farm Institute with one- to three-month internships, after which you can apply to stay on as an apprentice. And in California, organic walnut farmer Craig McNamara decided to use his farm as a living laboratory and started the California Farm Academy. His farm in Winters, California, is now the headquarters for the Center for Land-Based Learning.

How else can you learn? Talk to farmers selling their produce at your local farmers market. They might be delighted to have an "apprentice" come out and help. In fact, another clever California farming outfit, the

Pie Ranch in Pescadero, offers work days for ordinary folks so they can experience life on a farm. Leave your dogs at home and bring a pair of heavy gloves, they advise. After a few hours of helping out, you can attend a potluck dinner and traditional barn dance.

RESOURCES

www.essexfarminstitute.org

www.landbasedlearning.org

www.pieranch.org

Learn to Cook Another Language

Do you have a favorite international dish? Something you seek out at restaurants around the country and around the world? Your quest for the best ramen, perhaps, or a lifelong hunt for amazing French bread. Do you lie awake at night lusting for a great chicken mole? If so, you can learn to cook these dishes yourself in their native setting, improving both your language skills and culinary expertise.

As an example, let's take mole, the famed Oaxacan dish from that region of Mexico. Where could you learn to cook a mole like the ones you dream of? At Casa de los Sabores Cooking School.

After deseeding the chiles, toasting them in a comal, and grinding other ingredients into the paste that forms the base of the sauce, how will you ever be able to eat this in a restaurant again? You won't. You will be making it yourself from now on and thinking of the steps in Spanish as you do.

Or perhaps you long for Italian: the food, the country, the language. Speakandcookitalian.com, run by Lingua e Sapori, has a full list of events in the northern New Jersey and New York area. If you are ready to go farther afield, try the French cooking programs at École des Trois Ponts in southeast France that combine pastry skills with language skills.

RESOURCES

www.casadelossabores.com

www.speakandcookitalian.com

www.3ponts.edu

Become a Master Fermenter: Make Your Own Pickles, Beer, Bread

The farm-to-fork movement is everywhere, but how can you participate if you have no farm? You do have a kitchen, and perhaps a garage, in which you can ferment. Let's call it ferment-to-fork, where you can take pride in stepping up your kitchen skills and mastering one of the oldest methods of preservation in the world.

If at first you don't succeed… well, you know the rest. If you weren't able to get to that goal this time—whether it was baking a perfect loaf of bread or saving the money for a month-long stay in a Paris apartment—keep going. Why give up now? Maybe the next time you bake bread it will work. Maybe the next time you save some extra money it will put you over the top for that trip to France.

What can be produced through fermentation? A wonderful assortment of things… beer, for one thing. But you don't have to plunge right into a hobby that will require lots of expensive gadgets and gizmos. You can learn slowly by first mastering a recipe for refrigerator pickles. The PickYourOwn website offers simple recipes that only require basic kitchen skills. Make up a batch a few days before your next barbecue.

Tom Rotelli, a frequent fermenter, believes that "to employ fermentation is a leap of faith bordering on religion. To brew is human…to ferment, divine!" You can make cheese, yogurt, pickles, kimchi, and once you are confident of your yeasty skills, why not make some wine? Before investing in expensive specialized equipment, see if there is an amateur winemaking club in your area that you can join and have access to their equipment.

> **RESOURCES**
>
> www.pickyourown.com
>
> *Fresh & Fermented: 85 Delicious Ways to Make Fermented Carrots, Kraut, and Kimchi a Part of Every Meal* (Julie O'Brien and Richard J. Climenhage, Sasquatch Books, 2014)

Harvest Wine Grapes in France (or Work in a Vineyard)

Have you daydreamed for years about helping to bring in the grapes during harvest? Many a movie has featured idyllic scenes of bandana-clad workers in the vines, carefully cutting each bunch of grapes lest they be bruised and harm the wine. Can you really work in a vineyard? Yes, you can. But here is the hard fact—it is an undertaking for the young and strong. And it helps if you speak French.

The two websites listed here have information but seem geared toward college students looking for an adventure. If you're a mature adult with a fondness for wine, you may be better off making friends with your local winemaker and hinting that you'd just love to come around in the fall and lend an extra hand. Remember, you won't get what you want in life unless you speak up and ask for it, even with wineglass in hand.

RESOURCES

www.pickingjobs.com/france/grape-picking-jobs-in-france

www.apcon.nl

Make Your Own Customized Coffee

We don't all wake up the same way in the morning. Some people spring right out of bed, while others take their time. Maybe our coffee should also be customized according to our own particular styles. Rather than just grabbing whatever beans are on offer at the local grocery, you can create your own custom blend.

It could be as simple as buying two different kinds of roasted beans, one dark and one light, pouring the beans into a bowl and stirring the two types together before repackaging the blended

Longing for a house continually filled with beautiful bouquets? Instead of spending the money to achieve the look you seek, perhaps you could arrange a trade with a friend who has a lovely cutting garden. What could you do for her in exchange for flowers once a week?

beans. Or it could be more complicated. You could buy your own small roaster and experiment with green beans until you find a roast just to your liking. Or you could talk to a local coffee bean roaster about what you like and perhaps they could be persuaded to create it for you.

This may seem like a small thing to add to your bucket list, but remember, your life is unique and yours to shape and, more importantly, enjoy. Make every effort—even little ones like this—to create it to your liking.

Follow the Pie Rules of Conduct

So, I like pie. My theory is that the best pie is found in little roadside cafes and diners around this vast country. I keep a pie journal as I travel, making notes and keeping info on the various pie palaces I've found. Hot tip: if you are ever in Donnelly, Idaho, make haste to Flight of Fancy Bakery, a combination pie shop and air charter service. The. Best. Anywhere. Over the years I developed what I like to call the Pie Rules of Conduct. Some of the rules are that I have to sit at the counter when I order pie, have a cup of black coffee along with it, and chat

Do you have a collection of some sort? Vintage creamers and sugar dishes? Kentucky Derby party hats? Whatever it is, put it to use. Never be afraid to use what you own. If you finally acquire something you have always longed for, don't leave it on a high shelf! You are not a museum curator; your life is not on display. Take a cue from designer Ralph Lauren. He collects rare and expensive cars, but when interviewed about his collection, he always likes to stress that he drives these cars. He doesn't just park them in a showroom and admire them.

up the waitress who serves me. Ask about her life, ask about her town, her kids. Yes, it is always a woman who brings the pie.

By eating a piece of homemade pie in an unfamiliar town on what might be an unfamiliar road, I get the chance to meet interesting people and hear about lives different from my own. Get out there and talk to strangers—a piece of pie could be the makings of a delicious afternoon. Maybe cupcakes motivate you to hit the road. Or great barbecue. Would the search for the best grilled cheese sandwich in your state send you out the door? Think of a dish you love and get out there.

RESOURCES

www.roadfood.com

www.dessertjunkies.com

Try a Meatless Monday and Cook Up Something New

Give up meat one day a week? What kind of bucket list item is that? Who yearns to go meatless? Actually, some people do. (And many doctors are yearning for us all to give it a try.) It might be a small step toward changing your diet for the better. It is a simple idea—just have vegetarian meals on Mondays. That's it, no other rules or requirements. Just a clever slogan—Meatless Mondays—to remind you of the purpose.

Mark Bittman, food writer for the *New York Times*, took his eating habits one step further and decided to be what he calls "VB6." That stands for "Vegan before 6 p.m." So while some folks are committed vegans or vegetarians, and others are experimenting with skipping meat one day a week, he was embracing the idea that any meal before 6 p.m. would be vegan. You can find his philosophy in a book of the same name. Think about trying one of these methods, if only to improve your health and ensure that you'll get to do more of the exciting things on your bucket list.

RESOURCES

VB6: Eat Vegan Before 6:00 to Lose Weight and Restore Your Health (Mark Bittman, Clarkson Potter, 2013)

MAKE YOUR MARK:
Irresistibly Fun DIY
Activities and Skills

Find Your Own Food

So much ink is being devoted these days to the concept of "farm to fork." Very chic. But can you skip the farm and get right to finding food for your fork? Definitely. Few things are as elemental and yet intensely satisfying as the experience of gathering your own food. I don't mean getting it from a grocery store or from someone else's efforts, like some poor sous chef slaving away in a hot restaurant kitchen, but rather going out into the field, into the forest, or down to the shore to get it yourself.

Hunting, fishing, and foraging bring us back to our earliest days as a species and remind us to appreciate the

Although I didn't grow up in a fishing family, a few years back I began crabbing in Puget Sound with thrilling and delicious success. How did I learn? I bought a book called *How to Catch Crab*. I'm not always in the Pacific Northwest though, so the fastest way to get my own food from nature is to walk out the door and pluck dandelion greens from the back lawn. Wash them thoroughly, then boil for three or four minutes. Drain and chop them into small pieces, and add them to rice or anything that you think needs a pop of flavor and color. And then for fun, casually mention to your guests that they are eating weeds.

alternatives. Eating was pretty much a hit-or-miss experience for millennia. Some days the fishing was good. Some days the game was slow enough to catch. Some days you stumbled into a field of ripe berries and other edible plants. And some days your daily search turned up nothing. You won't take things for granted once you've had that experience.

Live in the city away from the natural world? If you are an urbanite, you can still feed yourself. If you live near the coast, grab a shovel and head to the shore when the tide is low to dig for clams. Lower a baited crab ring off a dock. Join up with a fishing charter. If the ocean is nowhere nearby, you can take a class in identifying and harvesting native edible plants. And never be afraid to ask someone more experienced than you are for help. Outdoor people love to share what they know, so speak up and ask for help and advice.

Hank Shaw, food blogger and forager extraordinaire, says in his book *Hunt, Gather, Cook*: "We live in an edible world. It's all around us, if you look closely... Knowing your plants and animals, learning to forage and fish and hunt, and then understanding what to do with what you have found is, for many, a deeply spiritual experience."

Keep an eye out for fruit trees in unusual places, such as hanging over the edge of a fence in an alley or forgotten in the corner of an empty lot. Native Californian George Basye grew up around fig trees and keeps an eye on an ancient tree that no one claims at the far end of a grocery-store parking lot. "When they are ripening I am there two to three times a week. No better breakfast than a fig you picked yourself." Watch for wild berries on your summertime hikes. When you're picking berries, purple fingers and a stained shirt are signs of great accomplishment. Cobblers and jams will taste so much better than when they are made with fruit from your grocery store's produce section.

Once you start looking at the world around you, trying to spot what is free and edible, your perspective shifts and you may well be drawn into other related activities. Hank Shaw learned to hunt in his forties. Where might this new skill take you?

RESOURCES

www.eattheweeds.com

www.ediblewildfood.com

www.honest-food.net

Hunt, Gather, Cook: Finding the Forgotten Feast (Hank Shaw, Rodale Books, 2011)

Build It Big: Create Something of Lasting Value

"It gave me such a sense of accomplishment," Julie Howard said, "even if it didn't turn out perfectly." What filled her with such pride? She and her husband built a brick wall together.

Working with your spouse or children or a group of friends to build something is an unbeatable way to create something of lasting value. Whether you are putting together a stone wall in the garden, laying out a patio, or building a new deck, a clay pizza oven, or an outdoor shed, you will have built a structure that wasn't there before. It exists because *you* wanted it and you made it. Close your eyes and imagine some-one in your family pointing with pride many years from now to what you have done. Build something that your great-grandchildren can treasure.

George Bingham built a stone wall in his backyard with the help of his son, Ian. "I was the grunt guy, lifting and carrying," he said. "And Ian, he was the stone artist, arranging each one just so, filling in the gaps with smaller stones." No quick project, it took all summer. But now George can look out his kitchen window and see the wall every day, reliving the experience he had with his son so many years ago. "Sometimes it brings tears to my eyes," he said. "He's grown now and off on his own, but there it is, the wall we made together."

Open Your Own Bookstore

In decades past, owning a bar was a common romantic daydream. Perhaps it was fueled by our culture's obsession with *Cheers*. Then everyone wanted to own a coffee shop with its own small coffee-bean roaster and locally produced milk. Perhaps the popularity of *Friends* had something to do with this? Now, many daydreams have shifted toward the romantic idea of owning an independent bookstore. Is this a dream of yours? Running a small bookstore has never been an easy way to make a buck, but with fewer big chain stores, a touch of backlash against the online sellers, and the "buy local" movement, the number of independent bookstores in the country is on the upswing.

The American Booksellers Association helps encourage store owners. Every year the organization sponsors a Booksellers School with the consulting firm Paz & Associates where you can learn the basics or improve on the bookish skills you already have.

If the expense and responsibility of owning an actual shop and running it day to day doesn't fit your lifestyle or your pocketbook, why not put up a free library instead? Little Free Libraries were started in 2009 by a couple of guys in Wisconsin and have now spread to more than 15,000 around the world. For a few hundred dollars you can buy an already-made book box to put up in front of your house or business. Or you can download plans and build your own. And then decorate it any way you want!

How does it work? You get the library rolling by putting out books that you are happy to see others take for free. Ask your neighbors to add books they no longer want to the mix. Delighted passersby will notice your Little Free Library as they walk down the street, open the box's door to peruse the titles, and take whatever appeals to them. If they are from the area, perhaps they'll return and add some of their own books to be discovered by strangers. And it goes on and on… You get the pleasure and good karma of being the local literary spot without the headache of making the monthly rent. And rather than spending hours reshelving books and dusting, you can straighten up the library in minutes!

Stepping it up a bit, you could also start your own literary reading series or author reading series. Not every town has a bookstore or public library with an existing structure for visiting writers. So you can step into the void and make one happen. Start a Little Free Library author series on your own front lawn. Or stand and read the classics together one evening. Poetry. Famous speeches. The themes and topics are endless.

Who could have predicted that when Todd Bol of Hudson, Wisconsin, built a small wooden model of the one-room school-house his mother once taught in, filled it with books, and stuck it on a post on his front lawn with a sign reading "free books," it would become a sensation? His "Little Free Library" idea went from the simple goal of building community and sharing books with his neighbors in Wisconsin to 15,000 replicas created by others around the world in less than a decade. If you are pursuing an idea that you are passionate about, share it! Who knows where it could lead.

> **RESURCES**
> www.bookweb.org
> www.littlefreelibrary.org

Shift into a Higher Gear: Drive a Stick

You've read the articles about how to keep your brain sharp. They appear constantly in the newspaper and in various magazines targeted to, um, mature audiences. So you have already heard all of the ways to keep your brain young and agile as the years go by…crossword puzzles, foreign languages, or musical instruments. And yes, do as many of those as make you happy.

But is there a sexier, more dashing way to work your brain without seeming so sedate and mature? Why not go back to driving a standard shift transmission? A standard transmission lends itself to a more physical connection between driver and car. With shifter firmly in hand, you could be operating with the car, instead of just operating it.

Real estate developer Dain Domich explains why he is a devoted stick-shift man:

> *The interesting aspect about the manual gear box, the "stick shift," is it gives the driver freedom to play*

the engine. There is nothing quite like bipping the throttle and feeling the motor surge as the fuel ignites and it runs up through its natural power band. Every motor has its own rhythmic cadence… its own sweet spot. There is a particular exhaust note in every engine's power band that hits a vowel-like sound… Some have a murmur, some howl, and some hit a French horn note. Some just roar and rumble restlessly. The "stick" lets you play the instrument. Pity the confines of a motor harnessed to an automatic transmission like a horse hitched to a wagon, envying the spirited mustang's free-running gait.

Always a fan of cars with standard transmissions (I've had four over the years), in 2013 I bought a 1966 Jaguar sedan with not just a standard transmission, but also right-hand drive. Talk about needing to pay attention to what is going on while I drive! Every trip is an adventure and a serious mental workout. And yes, it totally beats doing the *New York Times* crossword puzzle every day as a way to keep my brain nimble.

Very few new cars come with a standard–shift transmission option, and nearly all in the American car market are automatic. Small sports cars like the Mazda Miata or smaller economy models like the Honda Fit are the exception, but seeking out a modestly priced car with a shifter on the floor is also an excuse to go back in time to the cars you admired and envied when you were younger. Was there a '65 Mustang you always envied in the next-door neighbor's driveway? Perhaps an Oldsmobile or even a Cougar? Being able to shift is a skill you should always have at the ready. Who knows when you might find yourself navigating hairpin turns on the Italian coast in a vintage Fiat? The car fan website BenchSeat Chronicles is always looking for stories from readers about their fondest car memories. Perhaps you have one or two to share. Or will have, once you take up driving around town with your new stick shift.

RESOURCES
www.benchseatchronicles.com

You're On! Be in a Professional Opera

Envy the folks who have taken part in a live performance of some sort but feel like you don't have enough talent to pull it off yourself? Perhaps there is a role for you after all…in the background of a scene.

San Francisco Opera keeps a file of applications of folks who'd like to be in the background of a major

I took a class that San Francisco Opera offers in their Overture program and was surprised to find myself on a Monday night in a room full of other adults. Somehow, I thought I might be the only one actually interested in the topic…but no. Fifty people wanted to learn how opera "works." We wrote librettos and listened to young composers play and sing the words we'd just hammered out. We learned what the lives of the musicians are like in the pit and how the costumes are made. It was a delightful behind-the-scenes look at a world so few of us ever get to enter. I will never watch opera again without wondering who painted the scenery and how many singers have worn that one costume over the years. And at the end, they passed out applications to be walk-on, nonsinging supernumeraries!

production. These small roles are called supernumeraries, or "supers." The application is on their website, or you can email supers@sfopera.com for information. The application asks for a recent head shot and wants to know if you have had musical training or theatrical classes. And your measurements, so they will know whether you can fit into the already existing costumes. (Operas rent them from whomever owns the actual production. They seldom make everything for every opera.)

Keep an eye on the announced schedule to see what operas are being performed in upcoming seasons. Not every opera needs a large group of people

THE BIG BUCKET LIST BOOK

milling about for a village scene or dancing at a wedding. An opera like *War and Peace*, on the other hand, needs more supers than seems possible. The Met put out a public call for supernumeraries when they mounted that production in 2007 because they needed more soldiers for the battle scenes! Check with your local opera production company to see what they are up to and the process by which they fill super roles.

RESOURCES

www.sfopera.com

Develop Your Own Line of Food Products

For some of us, the idea of opening a restaurant has a great deal of bucket-list appeal. "One of these days… I will serve up my grandmother's famed ravioli… I will show the world how the best pie is made… I will wow my customers with my own secret formula for a well-seared steak." We all have favorite types of food around which our dream restaurant would be built.

But opening a restaurant isn't cheap and, in most circumstances, is highly risky. Go for it if you have money you can afford to lose, but if that doesn't describe your bank account, are there other ways to feed your need?

One of the biggest costs is a commercial kitchen, one that the health department deems worthy of serving food to strangers. If your dream involves one family recipe you'd like to share with the world, you can rent time in a commercial kitchen to prepare it and then sell it at farmers markets and food festivals. Pasta sauces, mustards, vinegars, and many family barbecue recipes are made and marketed this way.

If selling your food in bottles and cans doesn't satisfy your longing to serve an entire meal, perhaps you can offer to host a dinner party in your home as a charity auction item. It will give you the same experience of serving your food to strangers for money (although the money goes to the charity, with you assuming the cost of food preparation as your donation), and you will be able to do it in your own home.

Become an Art Curator

Owning an art gallery sounds posh, doesn't it? It also sounds like a difficult way to make money or an easy way to lose it. But if your dream is to be the one who chooses the artists and promotes the art, there are ways to make that happen in your life.

A phenomenon called ONO, or One Night Only, is a popular way to hang art outside a formal gallery setting. You could turn your own house or apartment into an ONO gallery simply by taking down what you have hanging on your walls now to create a blank canvas and removing some of the room's furniture to create better flow. Approach the artists you admire about doing a limited-time frame showing and art reception, hang the art and send out the invites, and presto, you are the owner of your own personal art gallery. If you succeed on your first try, do it a few times every year and create a regular event in the art community.

Don't want strangers in your own space? Perhaps there is a vacant building or office space whose owner would let you use it for a limited time. Be brave and ask the owner. They might be delighted with the prospect of hundreds of people coming to their building and view it as a marketing opportunity.

Attend Jewelry School at Van Cleef & Arpels

Do you love high-end jewelry? Are you curious about how artisans like Fabergé or Cartier created all those glittering trinkets? The French jewel house Van Cleef & Arpels recently opened its gilded doors to the public in a small way by allowing a select few to peek behind the scenes. L'École Van Cleef & Arpels gives aficionados the chance to explore the secret world of jewelry in Paris, "enabling enthusiasts to become enlightened amateurs." Classes are also held throughout the year in Paris and less often in places like Hong Kong and New York. The Paris classes and lectures are held in French and in English on topics such as "Symbols and Power of Jewels," "The Story of Talisman Jewels," and "Art Nouveau," as well as a more in-depth, behind-the-scenes look at Van Cleef & Arpels itself. Take a look at the schedule, and if you are going to be in Paris anyway, why not attend one of these unique classes?

On a far smaller (and less expensive) scale, there are countless places to learn the basics of jewelry making. Art schools, community college classes, craft stores, and bead stores all offer classes to get you started in developing your own unique bejeweled look.

RESOURCES

www.lecolevancleefarpels.com

Create Your Family's Memoir

So often we stop and think, "If only I had asked my grandmother for her recipe for apple pie. I've never tasted another just like it…" or perhaps the occasional, "I really should have written down those family stories my dad told me at the beach…" Now is your chance to make sure your own children never have those regrets. Get writing now.

This is an amazing time to put together a family memoir project, because there are so many ways to make a permanent record of your thoughts, pictures, and precious family lore. Should you put it together in a book? No problem. With print on demand, you can order just a handful of copies, one for each family member. Should it be a film? Easy. It can be done with an iPad, a smartphone, or a GoPro camcorder, or you could hire a professional to help you. A slide show of family photos with voice-over to describe who is in the picture and what is going on? Simple to do. A child could do it. (Really, they could.)

Imagine future generations of your family being able to access your thoughts and memories. Keep that image in mind as you work on your project. What better incentive could there be than to communicate with the future?

Live like Martha Stewart for a Month

How's this for a challenge? Try to live like Martha Stewart for a month. She publishes her calendar every month in the front pages of *Martha Stewart Living* magazine. The month of April looked like this a few years back: April 3, "service lawn mowers and sharpen blades." You could do that, right? Go out in the garage and make that the task for the day. Then on April 8, you could be like Martha by making it your task to "clean out car; schedule spring maintenance." Doable, totally.

Every other day or so she makes small notations about cardio or strength training, which you could do on those days, knowing that as you exercised, your buddy Martha was hard at work too. The task for April 19 is "bake lemon cake." Yum. Martha's calendar is also filled with the things she is going to do in her yard, like "plant a linden tree in honor of Arbor Day" and "rototill gardens." Wouldn't you feel in sync and on top of things if you were doing those things at the same time? You might have to be creative on the days she is riding her horse or speaking at a luncheon, but you could find similar things to do.

Why even try? Just to see if you could. Go ahead, pick a month. Maybe when the thirty days are up, you'll be running your personal lifestyle empire!

Found a Festival

Not happy with the festivals held in your area or wishing one specialized in whatever aspect of art, music, dance, or literature appeals to you? Well, start your own.

WordWave, a Lake Tahoe literary festival, grew out of two women's passion for books and desire to create a new and different way to celebrate them. Burning Man was started on Baker Beach in San Francisco by a man who built large bonfires and invited his friends to join him.

Betty Lucke led the Medieval Fantasy Festival for many years and put her expertise to work in a book called *Festival Planning Guide: Creating Community Events with Big Hearts and Small Budgets*. She covers the steps and pitfalls, which will help you on your journey to opening day.

Get out there and make it happen. Think of a catchy name. Buy yourself the domain name. Start telling everyone that you are putting together a new festival, and ask for their help and support. Soon you will be so deep in it that there is no backing out…and perhaps years from now we will all be talking about the amazing annual festival that *you* created!

RESOURCES

Festival Planning Guide: Creating Community Events with Big Hearts and Small Budgets (Betty Lucke, Spearmint Books, 2013)

"You will never do anything in this world without courage. It is the greatest quality of the mind next to honor."

—ARISTOTLE

Sail Away at a Wooden Boat Festival

Wooden boats bring to mind romance, allure, and adventure for many of us. But they are also costly to buy and maintain. Who wants to polish all that brass and teak anyway? Better to stroll around a dock and admire the beautiful boats for which other people pay the upkeep.

On the West Coast, Seattle and Lake Tahoe have famed wooden boat festivals, as does Washington's Port Townsend. That city hosts the largest wooden boat show in North America every September. In the Midwest you will also find many, including the Les Cheneaux antique wooden boat show in Michigan's Upper Peninsula. Or you might try Louisiana for the annual wooden boat show on Lake Pontchartrain.

Keep up with your favorite city. I have a "Today in Paris" app on my iPad that lets me know the weather, the major cultural activities, and tons of offbeat events going on around town. It helps me feel like I might leap on a plane at any moment to catch one of these performances.

If walking the piers and admiring the gleaming boats puts you in the mood to sail or drive one, where can you rent? One possibility is in Seattle at the Center for the Wooden Boat. Up in Canada, you'll find the Muskoka Launch Livery in Port Carling, Ontario.

RESOURCES

www.cwb.org

www.muskokalaunchlivery.com

www.cwb.org/events/festival/

www.laketahoeconcours.com

www.nwmaritime.org/events/wooden-boat-festival/

www.woodenboatfest.org/

Designate Your Own Meditation Room

Everyday life can be overwhelming sometimes. Noisy. Stressful. Crowded. Bright. Wouldn't it be wonderful to have your own quiet place? A room painted in a soothing color, with soft and welcoming furniture, scented candles, and a sound system to block out extra noise and play only quiet tones you can relax to. A yoga mat. A meditation pillow. Ahhh, you feel better just picturing such a place.

Not everyone has the extra space at home though, so how can you carve out a meditation area from what you have? Is there a quiet corner of the garden that can be put to use? A way to build a secluded area in the garage? Can you give up something to free the space? Even a nook between a couch and a wall works.

But what if you really have no place to go? Create a room within a room for yourself. Erect a small pop-up tent that you can decorate inside with cushions and scarves or something that makes it feel soothing. A place where everyone else in your life understands you are to be left alone for the next thirty minutes. If you don't want to go to all this effort, you can just turn your living room or kitchen into a temporary meditation area. Keep a box filled with the right accessories, and claim the room for your meditation space at times. Light the candles, sit on your meditation pillow, turn on some soothing music, and block the world out.

"Life is a blank canvas, and you need to throw on it all the paint you can."
—DANNY KAYE

.... ✱ ....

LIFE IS LEARNING:
Must-Know New Skills

Sail with the Big Boys

Big boys and big girls sail big boats. But if you didn't grow up with one docked off the end of your family's pier in Rhode Island, how are you ever going to gain the skills you would need to captain one yourself?

Petroleum engineer Eric Paulson looked longingly at large sailboats for years, until he decided to take time off and dedicate himself to learning to operate one with confidence. He was preparing for a retirement that he hopes will include a great deal of time under sail. "I had a small catamaran when I was younger, so taking up sailing again in a serious way helps me connect with my youth, the wind, and the sea." And as a person who likes challenges, he appreciates the complex play that sailing involves.

Once you have the skills, what can you do with them? Buy a boat if you have the cash, or rent one to sail with family and friends now that you have the proper skills and training.

To find a sailing school, look for one that specializes in the kind of boat you dream of sailing. But if you have never sailed before, you will have to start small. Very small. You might be in a class with young children, but hey, soon enough you'll be moving to bigger boats while they have to go inside and do their homework.

Island Dreamer Sailing School in Florida specializes in couples classes. Not only can you learn to sail together, but you can also acquire some of the skills you'd need to live aboard a boat together. Eric joined the Marina Sailing Club, which has six different locations around Southern California.

RESOURCES

www.island-dreamer.com

www.marinasailing.com

> "I love to sail on forbidden seas and
> land on barbarous coasts."
> **—HERMAN MELVILLE**

Around and Around You Go: Drive a NASCAR Car

NASCAR is one of the biggest sports around, attracting huge crowds to the stands and even larger viewing audiences. Are you a major NASCAR fan? Does the idea of driving one of those cars fill you with excitement? If that's what you want, the opportunity is closer at hand than you might think.

The Dale Jarrett Racing Adventure offers racing experiences at a number of tracks around the country, from Talladega Speedway to the Chicagoland Speedway and points in between. Something to consider before pursuing this—you do need to be slim and nimble enough to slide into the driver's seat through the window. There are no doors on a race car! Instructors will walk you through the hand signals you need to understand as you whiz by the pit crew, teach you how to safely enter and exit the track, and then away you go...

The cost of three laps around one of the tracks is fairly reasonable, around $200. The price goes up from there, with the chance to drive forty or sixty laps priced in packages north of $2,000. Keep an eye on your credit card bill, because sometimes this kind of opportunity can be had by cashing in your points.

Rick Gorsline described his experience behind the wheel at an Arizona track like this:

It was early with the sun just peeking over the horizon. I was headed for the Rusty Wallace Racing Experience and my chance to drive with no speed limit. I drove there that morning at street legal speed, savoring the vision of myself at the Phoenix International Raceway, following in the tire tracks of the legends of NASCAR with a big grin on my face. But my emotions were a roller coaster. After I arrived and had an hour-long training session that included how to eject in a crash (which occur almost daily) and dressed in a red flameproof jumpsuit, I had a serious case of the jitters and my adrenaline was out of control.

I rode my first three laps with a trainer who pointed out the line and braking points on the curves with hand signals. It was too loud to talk.

Then it was my turn. I crawled in feetfirst through the driver window. At age seventy-one, it was no small feat. I attached the seat belts: crotch, chest, shoulders, waist, neck brace. I got the signal. Time for me and my Budweiser number 6 to enter the track. Sixteen laps with 500 horsepower. Bright-colored cars rocketed by, the noise deafening, and I joined them.

It was much more of a rush than zip-lining. More like skiing fast and slightly out of control. Every lap I tried to increase speed. I didn't go as fast as the pros, but I'm glad I was there that morning. The drive home at seventy mph felt like tortoise speed.

Sound like something you'd be up for? Then go for it.

RESOURCES

www.racingadventure.com

www.racewithrusty.com

Pick Up and Play: Take Up a New Instrument

Recent findings suggest that classically trained musicians succeed on a far larger scale than most people do, even in nonmusical ways. There is also evidence to suggest that learning to play an instrument helps stave off Alzheimer's. So what are you waiting for? Pick up something and play!

Even if you were a reluctant musician back in the day or didn't play as a child but always wanted to, it's never too late to learn an instrument. And now you are ready to practice without your parents nagging you about it. Who knows where it might lead? You could even join an amateur symphony.

Mark O'Connor, a prominent composer and performer, has this message for anyone thinking about taking up the violin:

I encourage adults of any age to take up the violin with its rich source of tunes, stylistic diversity, rhythm, harmony, creativity, and improvisation. We see a lot more interest especially among people with kids going off to college. If you have time and some funds for a hobby, the beautiful wooden instrument is a marvel even to hold, besides learning about the craft behind the making of the instrument and the stories it tells you as you begin to bow its strings. I can't think of a better instrument for an adult beginner or an adult who wishes to begin again now that years have been added in between.

Mark has developed his own string learning program, the O'Connor Method, with an emphasis on learning American music. "The pieces in my book series are especially powerful as they tell the history and story of Americana and its multiplicity of culture and ideas. Even the beginning tunes are professional tunes that can be added to and shaped by individual expression. An American school of string playing is on the rise and people are starting to take notice."

Seeking an unusual Valentine's Day gift, I asked a professional musician friend to give me a few lessons on the recorder. She taught me the basics and then together we studied the sheet music to Elvis Presley's "Love Me Tender." I gave it a shot, practiced it over and over, and then performed it for my partner on the big day. Did he recognize the song? Well, not really, but when I told him afterward what it was, he was quite touched by my attempt. Time to keep practicing…

RESOURCES

www.oconnormethod.com

Retired radio station owner Susan Carson has become so devoted to her piano lessons that when she travels, she calls ahead to discuss gaining access to a piano in the hotel so that she can maintain her practice schedule. Not only is she a better pianist as a result, but she can lay claim to having "performed" all over the world!

Learn a Secret Language

Ever wanted to learn a secret language that is understood by only a few select folks around the world? Sounds like a Harry Potter novel, but it exists. *Lernu!* Huh? That means "learn" in Esperanto, a language created in the twentieth century to unite world cultures and spread world peace. From the Esperanto Circle of Santa Barbara to the Esperanto Society of New York and almost everywhere in between, somewhere someone is trying to master this style of communication.

Benny Lewis, the self-proclaimed Irish Polyglot, believes that two weeks spent trying to learn Esperanto will pay off in a big way in helping you learn any other language. Why? "Because it's easy," he says. "And the more languages you learn, the easier it is to learn a new one." You can find his philosophy and guidance at his website.

Cook Your Way through a Cookbook

Were you envious when you first saw *Julie & Julia*, the true story of a young woman who attempted to cook every recipe in the Julia Child masterpiece, *Mastering the Art of French Cooking*? Oh, and she vowed to do it all in one year.

If you love to cook, how about something like that as a personal challenge? Rather than setting such a rigid timeline, perhaps just vow to cook one recipe a week out of the cookbook of your choice for as long as it takes you to get through it. Think how happy your family and friends would be if you announced a plan to cook your way through *The Cake Bible* or perhaps one of Alice Waters's Chez Panisse tomes and share your creations with them.

For even more fun, choose a classic that you always meant to spend more time with or a cuisine that has

Ready to cook through a book? Here are a few that will keep you busy discovering new recipes and flavors:

◆ *Essentials of Classic Italian Cooking* (Marcella Hazan, Knopf, 1992)

◆ *Saveur: The New Classics Cookbook: More Than 1,000 of the World's Best Recipes for Today's Kitchen* (Editors of *Saveur* magazine, Weldon Owen, 2014)

◆ *Food Truck Road Trip—A Cookbook: More Than 100 Recipes Collected From the Best Street Food Vendors Coast to Coast* (Kim Pham, Philip Shen, and Terri Phillips, Page Street Publishing, 2014)

◆ *The America's Test Kitchen Cooking School Cookbook* (Editors at America's Test Kitchen, Boston Common Press, 2013)

always intrigued you. Moroccan? Russian? Sushi? You could even organize a group of friends to do it with you—and you don't all have to be in the same place. For example, a group of women around the country call themselves the Alpha Bakers and are working their way through *The Baking Bible*. They call the experience "a baking voyage through over 100 recipes." What will you call your culinary journey?

Attend Oxford

British accents seem to make people sound smart, and those who spent time at Oxford University sound even smarter, don't they? Relax. There is still time for you to achieve that same distinction. For the past forty-five years, the extension program of University of California, Berkeley, has run an adult learning program at Oxford.

These three-week, midsummer sessions on campus are billed for the "intellectually curious adult," and recent courses have been on topics like "Into the Vortex: Britain in the Interwar Years," "The Tudors: Myth, Performance, and Reality," and "Art and Power in the Age of Chaucer." Attendees actually stay in the famous old rooms of one of the oldest of the colleges and take meals in the ancient dining hall.

That said, this is not an inexpensive undertaking. The tuition is comparable to what you might have spent for your children to take a summer semester in college. But hey, it's Oxford!

Closer to home, if Harvard was ever on your go-to list, you can take extension courses there. Don't live in Boston? Use an extension course as an excuse to be a college student again and rent a room for a month or two.

RESOURCES

extension.berkeley.edu/oxford

extension.harvard.edu

Get Your Hands Dirty: Participate in an Archaeological Dig

Since 1992, ordinary nonarchaeologist folks have been able to help the pros on a site in Cyprus. Even actor Bill Murray has shown up to dig and sift. If being an archaeologist was your childhood dream, perhaps this is a chance to live it.

This is not an inexpensive undertaking; the price of the Exec-U-Dig program is about $10,000 for the week! But there is a small upside to the hefty price tag (beyond getting a really cool experience). Joan Breton Connelly, the program director for this New York University project, points out that the fee itself is a fully tax-deductible contribution. "Participants also pay for their room and board, which is not tax deductible," she says. "Pricing here varies according to the taste of the participants. Some wish to live with the team—this is quite reasonable (though we have no air-conditioning and few creature comforts); others wish to stay up the road at a four- or five-star hotel."

What is the actual experience like? Joan described it this way:

> Participants are full-fledged members of the Yeronisos team, traveling out by fishing boat to

the island at 6:00 a.m. each morning for a full day of digging. They receive careful training in correct techniques for using trowels, handpicks, dental tools, and brushes; the logic behind stratigraphic excavation and how to "read" the earth; as well as best practices in the removal, documentation, and conservation of finds.

We return to the mainland at 2:00 p.m. for a hearty lunch, siesta, and swim in the pristine, aquamarine Aegean Sea. Then off to the sherd tables at 6:00 p.m. for washing and sorting pottery fragments, working on the giant "jigsaw puzzle" of sherds that join into whole vases. The dig day comes to a close with a leisurely, candlelit dinner beneath the grape arbor, giving the team time to unwind, enjoy local wine, discuss the day's discoveries, and share adventure stories before heading off to bed.

Exec-U-Diggers also enjoy special team excursions to local museums, archaeological sites, monasteries, and nature preserves. This enables them to experience firsthand the richness of Cypriot cultural heritage and ecology, to hike the stunning trails of the Avakas Gorge and Akamas Peninsula, and to visit the Lara Bay Sea Turtle Conservation Station.

Restore an Object You Love

Using your hands, your creativity, your time, and your patience to slowly bring an old object back to life is tremendously rewarding. Whether it is an old house in need of restoration, a small piece of furniture in need of loving care and a new coat of wax, or a treasured family quilt that has begun to show its years, taking the time to get hands-on with a project is always time well spent.

Learning how to go about a major restoration project will bring new things into your life—new books, videos, and how-to television shows to acquire the skills you need; new people with the same interest as you begin to spend time in the aisles of the hobby, craft, or hardware store for the tools you need; and perhaps a whole new circle of friends if you start to take classes on your new interest.

Your fascination with restoration may begin to affect the places you travel, the music you listen to (music from the same era as the piece you are restoring might cheer you on in your task), and the topics of conversation with those around you. Just one simple step toward bringing something back to life could open a new door in your own.

"My mission in life is not merely to survive, but to thrive; and to do so with some passion, some compassion, some humor, and some style."
—MAYA ANGELOU

Learn a Long-Lost Skill for Today

Yesterday, tomorrow. Yestermorrow. A place where you can learn skills from the past that will help you in the future. This design/build school teaches more than a hundred different workshops on topics like traditional hand-tool chair-making, historic preservation, earthen oven building, straw-bale design, and timber framing.

The school was founded in 1980 in Waitsfield, Vermont, by a group of architects and builders who wanted to change the way we build houses and communities. The founders believed that building skills and architecture should be learned together seamlessly, in the hope that better design would emerge as a result. Students are of all ages and backgrounds, but these are not drop-in, casual, weekend courses.

The Art of Stone, for instance, runs from Sunday to Friday to teach students the design-and-build basics they need to build an arched entryway. An even more intensive experience is offered in a course taught in an abandoned village in Italy where the students spend fifteen days learning to preserve and restore historic masonry buildings in the Piedmont.

RESOURCES

www.yestermorrow.org

Drive a Real Train on a U.S. Railroad

Do your eyes grow misty when you see a train pass by? Do you long for the days of steam travel or the sound of a huge locomotive chugging by in the dark? What about actually driving that train yourself? You can at the Northern Nevada Railway, which has several programs that might wet your train whistle… from actually being the engineer with your hand on the throttle (and the chance to blow the whistle!) to working on the railroad as a jack-of-all-trades or volunteering on a train restoration project.

Other places need volunteers too. Steamtown National Historic Site in Pennsylvania sometimes looks for dedicated train lovers to help out there. And you may find another train site looking for volunteers closer to home.

RESOURCES

www.nnry.com

www.nps.gov/stea/getinvolved/volunteer.htm

Get Silly at Clown School

Juggling, tumbling, and other circus tomfoolery can be a welcome way to release everyday stress. No one knows that more than Wavy Gravy, a famed '60s figure who for decades has operated a summer camp that lets kids and adults be clowns.

Camp Winnarainbow is now in its fortieth year. Adults can sign up for trapeze lessons, magic, belly dance, and more. Located in California's Mendocino County, the camp offers sessions of just a few days or longer.

Maybe taking an improv class is what you need to be more relaxed while giving sales presentations. Or perhaps learning how to twist and

Not ready to try clowning? How about a visit to the Ringling Circus Museum in Sarasota, Florida? Established in 1948 in the same location as the winter home of the circus, the museum contains fascinating objects from the circus world such as John Ringling's private railway car, performers' wardrobes, vintage circus posters, and all types of circus equipment that was needed to keep the show on the road.

◆ www.ringling.org
/circus-museum

twirl on silk ropes above the ground will inspire you to go home and head back to the gym. Haven't played dress-up since you were a child? Camp Winnarainbow boasts a huge costume collection for your inner child.

Mooseburger Clown Arts Camp in Buffalo, Minnesota, is more focused on campers becoming actual clowns, whether amateur or professional. From balloon-animal skills to face painting, this is your complete clown learning course.

RESOURCES
www.campwinnarainbow.org
www.mooseburger.com/moosecamp/

CREATE AND INSPIRE:
Art, Film, Theater, and More!

Let Me Count the Ways... Become a Poet

Was there a poetry phase in your distant past? A year of high school when most of your time was devoted to penning tragic but romantic odes to a fellow student who—insert deep sigh here—was totally unaware of your existence? So many of us did this...and then, blushing, put away our adolescent attempts and went on to lead responsible, nonpoetic lives.

But how about now? Why not become a poet in this next phase of your life? Why not sit down and pen a romantic ode to your lifetime partner? Or an ode to the rosebush in your front yard, your trusty

Volvo, or perhaps the grower at the farmers market from whom you buy those amazing tomatoes.

How do you get started? Simple. Get out of the way of your own emotions. Instead of trying to make every word perfect, just write down everything that comes to mind. Pretend you are listening to jazz, and just jam with whatever comes out of your pen onto the page.

Do you need to share what you have written? Not if you don't want to. All writers keep something to themselves, so this can be your private stash. But if you do decide to brave sharing your poetry with your love interest, let him or her know what is going on. You don't want your efforts to be met with nervous titters.

Is love the only thing poets write about? Of course not. Write one about walking the dog. Write about composing your will. Write about making the bed. Drinking your coffee. Driving your car. Life is a poem. Write it down.

Take Up an Art and Create Often

Are your days of uninhibited, childlike creativity far behind you? Do you remember high-school art class fondly but haven't tried to draw, paint, or sculpt since then? What are you waiting for? It's time to dive back in and paddle around in your creativity. No one is watching; there are no grades to be earned; and you don't even need a teacher unless you seek one out.

A trip to your local art-supply store will give you ample inspiration and allow you to quietly dabble in whatever appeals to you most. Once you've got your creative mojo on, start looking for instruction through adult ed classes or museum activity days…or just do whatever feels right when the mood strikes. If you like what you make, put it out there for the world to see. Decorate your yard with your sculpture. Hang your paintings in the hallway. Send a drawing to your sweetie.

Art makes the world smile back at you. "It anchors you," says Ingrid Lundquist about her return to making art after an absence of thirty or so years. A painter in college, she now spends hours a week on her photography and has begun to travel for that sole purpose.

Award-winning cookbook and food journalist Elaine Corn took up ceramics because "it is the opposite of journalism. No deadlines. No facts. Mentors rather than editors. A world of shapes and colors and uses. The entire process calms me while keeping my hands and mind moving." Sounds very seductive. Elaine does point out one drawback though: "The only thing that art and journalism have in common are an audience and unreliable pay."

Start a Journal—and *Stick to It*

Finally, you have the time to journal! Yes, you've thought for a long time about developing the habit. But when? You were too busy with other things… but maybe now? Writing in a journal is an interesting and introspective habit, and best of all, it *doesn't* have to be as all-consuming as it might seem. Start by taking a few minutes at the end of the day to jot down things that were of interest to you. As you get in the swing of it, you will start to spend more time on your descriptions. A few words about a trip to the grocery store might lead to a paragraph describing the conversation you overheard in the pet food aisle and then to a longer recollection about a favorite pet from your childhood. Who knows where a journal entry could lead?

You don't have to write your journal in memoir form, of course. But close your eyes and imagine one of your descendants holding your handwritten journal in their hands years in the future. Wouldn't you have been delighted to stumble across something like that in your attic from someone in your own family? To have access to their inner thoughts and their immediate reflections on what was happening around them during events we only get to read about in history books?

So do it for the future. Get yourself a blank journal and sit down to write. The future is asking for your thoughts.

Bespoke Shoes: Custom Made Just for You!

"My number one bucket list item? Custom-made shoes," said Ingrid Lundquist, an event organizer who has helped to fulfill a dream or two for clients. "My job is all about other people, and having a pair of handmade shoes is a decadent treat solely for me."

Yes, solely for you. Shoes are a utilitarian item. Everyone needs them. They're used day in and day out. Splurging on an ordinary, functional object lifts it into the category of decadent treat. Actor Daniel Day-Lewis took this one step further and apprenticed himself to an Italian shoemaker for eight months.

But shoes are expensive, men's shoes particularly. For ladies, a pair of custom-made sandals might fulfill the dream and be less painful on the wallet. Jackie O strolled the streets of Capri in the '70s in slacks and a T-shirt, accessorized by a pair of Canfora sandals, and established a fashion trend that still exists today. Or if you want a less costly way to create your own pair of shoes, check out the ShoeDesignStudio website. Devoted to women's shoes, the site allows you to create your own style by working with an array of colors, patterns, styles, and heels.

RESOURCES

www.canfora.com

www.shoedesignstudio.com

Share Your Words at a Poetry Slam

If you are feeling comfortable in your poetic skin, why not take it up a notch and share your work with others? Participate in either an open-mic night or (gulp) even a poetry slam! Take a page out of one woman's book: "I'm not storing my dreams in a bucket," says Oakland-based writer Sheryl Bize-Boutte. "I'm pulling them one by one out of a Vuitton duffel!" With that image in mind, Sheryl has several big dreams, including winning the grand prize at a poetry slam night.

"They are usually populated by twentysomethings and you hear a lot of bad poems, but every so often something sparkles. And don't you think it is time for people our age to express ourselves in a different way?" In addition to wining the poetry-slam prize, she wants to read her poetry in a club in New Orleans as a way of celebrating her Creole heritage and because "it is the perfect funky, jazz-filled, zydeco-laced, sultry, creole-infused backdrop for my poems and stories."

How will Sheryl, or you, find a place to compete or just read? For one in your area (or, on second thought, maybe you want one that is *not* in your area), check your local arts listings online or in the paper to see who hosts poetry readings and open-mic nights for musicians and poets. Those places tend to have friendly crowds. For bigger stakes, such as entering a poetry slam, Poetryslam.com has a great map that shows where slams take place around the United States.

Become a Songwriter or Lyricist

Are you a secret Carole King or James Taylor? Strumming your guitar and softly crooning your own songs when you think no one is looking? Perhaps it's time to fulfill your dream and attend a songwriting camp to help your talent blossom to the fullest.

English guitarist and songwriter Richard Thompson runs a summer camp in New York's Catskills called "Frets and Refrains." And in eastern Tennessee John McCutcheon holds his annual camp. Professional recorder player Kathryn Canan recently attended his session, and describes it this way: "It was a week learning songwriting from one of my favorite songwriters. And yes, I'll be back for seconds of both the Southern cooking and the folk music. I've been attending music workshops for over twenty years, and writing workshops as well, but songwriting camp was a chance to step outside my comfort level and combine both interests."

"We were a varied group," she explains. "A pastor exploring her musical talents, a rock guitarist who wanted a chance for his own voice to be heard, a physician who wrote songs about biochemistry… Workshops like this bring amazing people together who love learning from each other and sharing their own gifts."

RESOURCES

www.fretsandrefrains.com
www.folkmusic.com/camp

Enter the Magic Castle

Is mastering a card trick to amuse your friends on your bucket list? What about pulling a coin from behind a young child's ear? Amateur magician, eh? Perhaps you'd enjoy a glimpse into the inner sanctum of the magical world...the famed Magic Castle. Professional magicians and entertainers belong to this elite Los Angeles mansion club, founded in 1963. This is a private club, make no mistake. The dress code is fancy, the atmosphere is elegant, the magic is endless, and yes, there is a way to get in...

Among the various membership categories is the choice of joining for thirty days for $250. That's a steep price to go out to dinner—and the dinners themselves are not inexpensive—but it is a way to get behind the doors of a famed gathering place. The Magic Castle website has detailed information on joining. If you hanker to know more about magic on the East Coast, call ahead and make a research appointment at New York's Conjuring Arts library. Historic books on magic tricks, old devices, and more are found here.

Not ready to set foot in such storied places? Check into magic classes taught in your area through adult education or online at the Free Magic School website.

Reenact History

Historic reenactments are everywhere. At Williamsburg, Virginia, Sutter's Fort in Sacramento, and every Civil War site in between, dedicated volunteers in authentic costume are working to convey the proper period.

Why do they do it? "Historic reenactments can bring important insights," says Sue Pearson. "Whether it's a medieval festival or a Civil War drama, when you step into costume and character you begin to understand not how different we are but how much the same. There is a sense of timeless community when you become part of living history. And from that community comes an understanding that we are all connected—then, now, and always."

Sue is new to the reenactment world. She participates in an all-female militia called the Nancy Harts in LaGrange, Georgia. Why? "My great-grandmother joined the real Nancy Harts during the Civil War at the age of fourteen. She and forty-five other armed women met the Union Army on the edge of their town, and their spirits were enough to convince the Union general to spare the town from destruction. When I put on that dress a hundred and fifty years later and lift a rifle, I feel Addie's strength flow through me and carry over into other parts of my life."

Is there a dramatic story from your ancestors that would draw you to reenact? Gold Rush explorers, early farmers, Revolutionary soldiers, or maybe you can even reach back in time to wear medieval clothes at a Renaissance fair in your area. Try being someone else in a different time period for a while, and who knows how that might influence who you are today.

Down in Front! Host Your Own Themed Movie Nights

Are you a serious movie buff? One who has watched *Cinema Paradiso* over and over with great longing, imaging yourself as the proprietor of an old-fashioned movie house in a quaint small town (preferably in Italy)? I can't help you with the small town in Italy, but building your own outdoor movie theater is a simple thing with today's technology.

In fact, you can curate your own themed movie series, inviting friends and family over to watch classics from your childhood or black-and-white film noir or only movies by French directors. The movie choice is up to you. Create a potluck dinner party around the film. Gladys Cornell and Steve Pass hosted their book group in their backyard one summer night for a showing of *The Motorcycle Diaries* and served Cuban sandwiches and other Latin dishes. Using a different occasion, Jasmin Iolani Hakes celebrated her birthday with an outdoor screening of *Hook* on her lawn. "Watching a movie outdoors makes everything magical," she says.

So what do you need to create your own outdoor movie theater? A screen, a projector, and a sound system. For high-end professional equipment that you can rent on a short-term basis, check out Fun Flicks, who will even rent you a popcorn machine. To buy equipment to make this a regular part of your summer life, see what is available used on Craigslist or eBay, or check the Backyard Theater website for equipment and setup ideas.

RESOURCES

www.funflicks.com

www.backyardtheater.com

Draw, Paint, or Create Art in a National or State Preserve

Does the idea of spending a week or two by yourself in the wilderness sound appealing? Just you and your art—poetry, essays, paintings, photographs. If you are serious about your craft, the parks might have a spot for you.

Some national parks run residency programs for artists and writers. These are very competitive programs, as you can imagine, and applicants come from around the world. The guidelines specify that established artists and writers can apply, without being very specific about what "established" actually means. For instance, Denali National Park in Alaska offers the use of a historic roadside cabin for ten days if they accept you. Check with your favorite national park to see if they offer a program.

Even if you aren't chosen for an official residency, set up your easel and get to work. Sit on a rock with your sketchbook or your journal. Let the scenery lead your creativity in new directions. Unpack your camera gear and climb on top of your car to get the perfect shot, à la Ansel Adams. He didn't have an official residency either, you know.

RESOURCES

www.nps.gov/subjects/arts/air.htm

Score a Role in a Big-Budget Movie

Hollywood. The film world. So very glamorous…so far removed from our everyday lives. Well, not really. Not if you are an extra in a big-budget film.

So how could you become one? Check with your state or county film commission for information on films in production in your town. The film commission should also be able to steer you toward reputable casting agencies that handle calls for extras. Beverly Lewis with the Placer County Film Commission says, "We get current information all the time on who is planning to shoot and when. Almost all films need extras."

And once you play a bit part (or just stroll through a frame or two) in a film that plays on the film festival circuit, then why not go? Imagine the excitement of sitting anonymously in the audience while the movie you watched being filmed is on the screen before you. Even if your scene never survives the final cut, hey, you were *there*. You were part of this in a way few others can claim.

Having once been an extra, you might get hooked and do it again. "I got a call to be one of thousands of extras in the Brad Pitt movie *Moneyball*. Those stands needed to be filled somehow," said Marie Vines. She'd connected with a casting company years before

A few years back my partner David and I spent a late-summer day at an estate in Tahoe as partygoers in a film scene. Hour after hour we pretended to drink champagne (a skill we have perfected in real life) while strolling in front of the camera from one part of the yard to another, or leaning in to have an animated conversation with another couple or two. All silent, of course. We just moved our mouths. And alas, the champagne wasn't real. But there we were on a real movie set, the camera operators, producers, and directors around us, the actual stars of the film sometimes seated at our table. Neither of us had ever done anything like that before, and although dull at times, overall it was a huge thrill. Fast-forward another summer and there we were seated on a big lawn, real champagne in hand, watching a private outdoor screening of "our" film. Check us out in *Last Weekend*, a film by Tom Dolby.

and was delighted and surprised to hear from them about the opportunity. So get on a list and wait for the glamour to descend.

Be Like a Boy Scout and Learn Basic Survival Techniques

Could you be a survivor? I don't mean on that TV show or even in the medical sense. But rather could you survive without the conveniences we rely upon in our everyday lives? You've seen the ads that doomsday suppliers run every so often with frightening messages about the coming collapse of modern society. Have you ever thought, "Maybe I should stock up on some canned goods. You just never know…"

Rather than feeding into paranoid fears about the collapse of civilized society in our lifetimes, why not develop the skill set that will give you a quiet sense of calm and the knowledge that, yeah, you actually do know what to do if the S#%^&*t hits the fan.

Get started by looking around your house. What will work? What will still be useful when the power goes out? Sure, we all experience ordinary outages from time to time, but what if the power was out for several days due to a natural disaster? What would your strategy be for heat? Light? Cooking? Water? Do you have basic camping gear on hand in case you need to evacuate the area for a while?

Some of the most useful skills sound like what we should have learned back in Boy Scouts:

Basic fire-building techniques.

Basic shelter-building techniques.

The ability to identify edible plants.

Emergency medical knowledge.

Ability to purify water.

Once you've learned these, you'll not only be sure you can survive whatever might happen, but you'll also feel more confident and able. Want to learn more? Websites like the ones listed here are filled with helpful articles on how to survive various disasters.

RESOURCES

www.backdoorsurvival.com

www.happypreppers.com

Create a Motivational File

To keep your life exciting and moving forward, there's nothing like committing to do something that you aren't really sure you can do. Scary. Run a half marathon? Write an award-winning essay? Build a wooden go-cart? You'll never know until you try, and the first step is filling out the application or entry form. Send it off, and then start worrying!

Why not keep a file marked "Apply Yourself" filled with somewhat frightening but possibly doable things? Whether the activity is physical, mental, or educational, try it out. If not now, when? Julia Berenson didn't consider herself a literary writer but nevertheless challenged herself to send an application to a monthlong writing fellowship on Cape Cod. "And a matter of days later I got a call saying I could come. I was stunned. Could be because I said I was available in the month of March, when no one else wanted to go there, but hey, they said yes!"

So apply yourself to a challenge. Fill out your application and hit Send. Who knows where it could lead you?

Make a Documentary

Ever watched a stirring documentary and thought to yourself, "Wow, I really should make a film about…" Fill in the blank with the topic that most interests you. Chances are, if something is a burning interest of yours, other folks out there have the same interest. Gather what you need to make your own documentary and get to work. But wait, isn't filming a documentary complicated and beyond the reach of most of us? Not anymore. As with so many things, technology is firmly on the side of the amateur.

"Technological advances have made it much more affordable to film a documentary," said author Richard Poe. A devoted kayaker, Richard was fascinated by the art of kayak rolling and, after learning it himself, felt others should be exposed to the idea.

There's something magical about rolling a kayak. You turn the boat upside down, then roll it back up again. It's like conquering death. After years of kayaking, I finally made up my mind that I was going to master this ancient skill of the Inuit people. Learning to roll was one of the greatest triumphs of my life. I wanted to share it. I knew that if I could convey even a small part of how it really feels to roll a kayak, I would be giving people a unique and powerful experience.

Up until recently, documentarians would have needed serious camera equipment. "Marie and I did all the shooting for *The Way of the Kayak* using six rented GoPro cameras fastened to two boats," Richard said. "The GoPro is so advanced, it practically runs itself. Then there's the iPhone. When the late Malik Bendjelloul ran out of money for his Oscar-winning documentary *Searching for*

Sugar Man, he finished shooting with an iPhone. And it worked!"

Richard and his wife, Marie, are still in the midst of the process. "What we completed is a five-minute trailer, which we posted on YouTube to promote the film. We tried to make the trailer a complete film unto itself, and it must have worked because most people don't even notice that it's a trailer." Check it out and be inspired to grab a GoPro and get to work on your own documentary. Richard's best piece of advice is this: "Pick a topic that you're truly passionate about. Your passion will drive the film."

RESOURCES

www.richardpoe.com/films/the-way-of-the-kayak/

www.desktop-documentaries.com

www.gopro.com

Revive the Art of the Handwritten Letter

Have you made it a habit to thank the people who have most influenced your life? The teachers, guides, pastors, parents, relatives, neighbors, bosses, friends who had a hand in guiding you toward where you are today? Expressing gratitude throughout the day is a wonderful exercise, but going back to seek someone out and send a handwritten letter is a transformative experience. Skip the emails, please; just detail how much their presence in your life has meant to you.

"One of my 'bucket list' items is to make sure I thank many of the people who have helped me along in this life," said musician Kathryn Canan. "Especially those who have no idea of their impact. I just learned that a cousin died unexpectedly at age sixty, far too young. That it can all end so suddenly without warning makes me even more determined to take advantage of opportunities that pop up in life and appreciate the people I care about."

GIVING BACK:
Make Your Mark

Run a Marathon

Is running a marathon too much of a clichéd bucket-list item? Not at all, because of the hard work you'd have to do to get ready. Many runners choose to join a training program to make sure they are properly prepared.

The Leukemia & Lymphoma Society began hosting marathons in 1988 and then developed a larger program to train the participants to ensure greater success and commitment. Over the years, Team in Training has grown into the largest endurance-sports training program in the world. It is so well regarded that many weekend athletes use it to train for other full or half marathons, as well as cycling and hiking events. The society even has an online TNT Flex option for runners who don't have time to sign up for the full commitment.

RESOURCES

www.teamintraining.org

Become a Citizen Activist

Is there a national issue or a social cause that keeps you awake at night? Maybe it's time to step in and try to make change on a large scale. In our democratic system, elected officials aren't the only ones who can affect change. As ordinary citizens, we can too.

Liza Long from Idaho has seen the journey from soccer mom to citizen activist in her own life:

On December 14, 2012, I was just a soccer mom with four children in Boise, Idaho. But I had a painful secret. While the nation shuddered in horror at the tragedy of Newtown, Connecticut, with twenty children and six educators dead, my heart ached for a boy and his mother. I decided to share my truth: my son was sick. We needed help. And no one would help us. My son was just thirteen, and already he had been in juvenile detention four times, hospitalized three times. After all those years, all those specialists, and an alphabet soup of incorrect diagnoses, we had no idea how to help him. I wrote these words on my blog: "I am Adam Lanza's mother."

The viral consequences of my essay were overwhelming. I was excoriated for talking openly about something that many critics said should be kept private: mental illness and violence. I quickly decided that advocacy trumps privacy, that I have nothing to be ashamed of, and that I will continue to speak up for my son and for the millions of families like mine who are still suffering in shame and silence. Since that day, I've testified to a congressional forum. I've spoken to numerous groups and given a TEDx talk about ending stigma. I wrote a book, The Price of Silence: A Mom's Perspective on Mental Illness, which describes the many ways our broken system fails children, families, and communities. But it also offers hope.

The best consequence of sharing my truth is that my son was finally diagnosed with bipolar disorder. Today, he is managing his condition, attending a mainstream school, and writing a book of his own. I'm still just a soccer mom in Boise, Idaho. But I've *learned that when soccer moms come together, they can change the world.*

What is your cause? Education? Poverty? Art in the school? What would you like to change about the world, the country, your state, or your community? Raise your hand. Get involved. Start a movement and watch it grow.

RESOURCES
www.citizen.org

Volunteer in National Parks

You love visiting our various national parks—the grandeur of Yosemite, the wildlife of Yellowstone, the quiet majesty of Denali. Why not hang out there awhile and see new sides of these parks? They welcome volunteers with open arms. From building trails to staffing an information booth or warning visitors away from rutting elk, you will become a true insider and value our parks even more.

Recent volunteer positions include a monthlong stint as a caretaker at the Yellowstone Overlook field campus, a map editor with the U.S. Geological Survey in Maine, or a bike patrol person on the Natchez Trace Parkway in Mississippi.

Find out what you can do for your country and enjoy our natural American wonders by visiting www.volunteer.gov and checking out how to help at your favorite national park. As it says on the website, "If you like people and care about our country's natural resources, the Forest Service needs you."

If a long stay in a national park isn't in the cards right now, chances are your local parks would love to hear from you. Budget constraints have cut into tasks like gardening and maintaining trails. Call your local parks department and ask if they need your help.

RESOURCES

www.volunteer.gov

Those Who Can, Teach Others: Share Your Skill and Inspire Others

Chances are that you know something someone else would love to know. A skill. A talent. It doesn't have to be anything fancy. Maybe you know how to coax bulbs to blossom out of season. How to host inexpensive dinner parties. How to potty train a cat.

So what can you do with your skill or knowledge? Share it.

Few feelings are as gratifying as teaching and seeing the "click" of understanding when your student gets what you want them to understand. And the satisfaction of knowing that you have passed on knowledge to someone who can use it and later teach it to someone else. That is how the world keeps working, one small piece of shared knowledge at a time.

How can you teach what you know to others? Check out Skillshare, a website that allows you to create a prerecorded video course that students can access anywhere, anytime. You can even take a course on Designing Your Course to better understand how to teach on the site.

Not ready to teach online to folks from all around the country? No problem. Just post a flyer advertising your class in your neighborhood, send an email to your friends and acquaintances, or put a notice on your Facebook page. If you have a skill or type of knowledge that others are interested in, students will appear. And you will experience the warm glow of knowing that you have been able to share information and knowledge that could improve someone else's life.

Been Meaning to Give Something Up? Do It!

We live in an acquisitive world. Buy this, buy that… and deep down we know that these things, no matter how wonderful, won't give us lasting happiness. But what about the opposite of acquiring—will that bring satisfaction or happiness? Perhaps you should consider a bit of deaccessioning. "Deaccession" is a fancy art collector and museum term for giving something up. Selling it. Giving it away. Doing without it from now on.

The idea of a bucket list is to achieve your goals one after another. Why can't one goal involve *not* doing something? Or actively stopping doing something that pains you. What causes you the most grief in your life? A friend? Maybe even a family member. Give them up and move on.

You might try giving up meat, sugar, or alcohol for thirty days and see how that makes you feel. Lighter. Freer. Physically. Mentally. Emotionally. You may find that whatever you gave up freed money and time for you to pursue another item on your list. And you

"Elegance is Refusal" is a quote variously attributed to Diana Vreeland or Coco Chanel. What should you refuse to do? Don't forget to include things on your bucket list that you never intend to do again. Take a job you hate. Sit through a movie you aren't enjoying. Fly cross-country in a middle seat. The *New York Times* asked readers what was on their "reverse bucket list," things they never wanted to do in their hometown of New York. Among the suggestions were:

- Share a cab with the Naked Cowboy.
- Spend a night in Penn Station.
- Emerge from the subway and have to ask directions.
- Ask Alec Baldwin for an autograph.

will have proven to yourself that you have the inner strength to live without.

Serve on a Grand Jury and Help Deliver Justice

Yes, we all cringe when the jury summons arrives in the mail. It's a natural reaction. But we know it is our civic duty so we respond. Truth be told, often it wasn't so bad, was it? In fact, being part of a grand jury can actually be fairly riveting. This can be a great way to experience our justice system and hopefully help people in the process.

Different from a regular jury, a grand jury is most often an investigative body whose purpose is to decide whether there should be a trial on the matter at hand.

In some counties, serving on a grand jury is through the jury summons system, so serving is not something you can actively seek out. In others, however, you can. You also don't have to have a background in law to serve on a grand jury. Communities that allow grand jury applicants are looking for people with a wide range of skills and backgrounds so they can achieve as balanced a perspective as possible. There's no point in having a grand jury made up of all attorneys or all accountants, for example.

Members serve terms ranging from six months to a year or more. Remember, the point is to delve deeply into a few matters and seriously examine an issue. "As a practical matter, it doesn't work if you have a full-time job," says Anthony Da Vito, a former grand jury member in California. "It is [sometimes] a year of your life. You need to keep a broad attitude about people and be able to engage in discourse. Serving on a grand jury will really give you an understanding about how government really works."

To find out if you can apply to be on a grand jury in your area, visit the website of your local courts system.

Help Create a National Park Larger than Yellowstone

Not that long ago, just a hundred and fifty years or so, the United States had huge areas of original prairie populated by thriving and diverse wildlife. A movement to re-create at least part of that is underway at the American Prairie Reserve in northeastern Montana. The goal is to acquire three million acres, a size that would rival the Serengeti in open space. Bison, antelope, bighorn sheep, prairie dogs, and other native species would roam freely. Another national park in the works, it seems.

Currently the project owns more than 275,000 acres of grasslands in the northern Great Plains. It is not easy to get there, requiring a drive of several hours by car from Billings, Montana, some of it on dirt roads. This is a project deep in development, not near its final stage.

You can help. By contributing, by volunteering for a month on a citizen scientist team, or by simply visiting to camp at Buffalo Camp, a rustic campground, or stay in one of the Kestrel Camp's swanky glamping (glamorous camping) tents, your efforts will help the organizers continue to acquire land and create more interest in the project. Help create a park larger than Yellowstone? Not since the days of Teddy Roosevelt has the chance been available, The *National Geographic* calls it "one of the most ambitious conservation projects in American history." So go and be a part of it.

RESOURCES

www.americanprairie.org

Be in the Olympics

Devoted to the Olympics every four years? Summer Games or Winter Games, you are there in front of the television, watching every event. What if you could actually be a part of the Olympics instead of merely a spectator?

An Olympics is an enormous undertaking that requires a vast corps of volunteers. From office jobs to greeters at the stadium, each of the Olympics has a great need for free help. Why not become one of those critical folks? Note that not only are these volunteer positions but you also need to pick up your own expenses along the way. That means getting yourself to the event, wherever it is being held, and then arranging and paying for your own housing

Can you help sponsor someone else's Olympic dream? A friend of mine in the Pacific Northwest played an integral part in helping subsidize Apolo Anton Ohno in his early training days. Is there a kid in your community who deserves a little financial backing? Imagine how you great would feel if you later saw them on the podium.

Once you've won a gold medal at the Olympics, what do you have left on a bucket list? Stephanie Trafton is gearing up for the Olympics in Rio, and yes, she does have a bucket list goal. "My first Olympics was in Greece, and I had fun but didn't win. My second Olympics was in Beijing, and I brought home the gold. London? There was huge pressure as I was the reigning gold medalist, and I didn't pull it off a second time. So for my last Olympics I want to try to have a complete experience. I want to have fun being an athlete at the Olympics but balance that with the seriousness of going once again for a medal." Any nonathletic bucket list items for Stephanie? "Hunting in New Zealand with my husband."

during your volunteer stint, as well as taking care of your own meals.

You can volunteer more locally for time trials and other tryouts that might occur in your area. Keep tabs on what is needed at the Team USA website.

The importance of volunteers is central to the Olympics experience, track-and-field gold medalist Stephanie Trafton points out. "Volunteers are part of the action and are having their own authentic Olympic experience even if they aren't athletes. They are a big part of the competition." Stephanie won gold in the women's discus-throwing event in Beijing. "Volunteers were everywhere," she said. "I never even had to reach out to open a door for myself. They were there to do it for me. It was something to see all of these people, so proud that their country was hosting the Olympics on the world stage."

RESOURCES

www.teamusa.org/careers/volunteers

www.rio2016.com/volunteers/

Dig Up a Fossil

Harboring a Jurassic Park fantasy, are we? It may be easier than you think to become the bespectacled paleontologist with the battered and dusty wide-brimmed hat, focusing on fossilized bones. The Page Museum in downtown Los Angeles, more commonly known as the La Brea Tar Pits, uses volunteer help for much of what it does. Many thousands of years ago, saber-toothed tigers, woolly mammoths, and various other prehistoric creatures wandered over to drink from what turned out to be a sticky tar pit. They got trapped, and now we're the scientific beneficiaries of their well-preserved skeletal remains.

To help out with the fossils, you need to be more than sixteen years old and able to commit at least one full day a week for a minimum of three months. What a great reason to rent a place on the beach for a few months and get to work helping to sort matrix (asphaltic and earthen material encasing the fossils). "Lab volunteers do the majority of the day-to-day preparation of fossils from our current excavations," according to the website. "The work they contribute is invaluable."

A few states over, Crow Canyon Archaeological Center lists opportunities for lifelong learners on their site, not only for their campus in southwest Colorado, but also for archaeologically themed scientific tours to places like Olmec and Mayan ruins in Mexico or archaeological sites in Crete.

RESOURCES

www.tarpits.org/la-brea-tar-pits

www.crowcanyon.org

Become a Theater Producer

You saw the Mel Brooks movie and took in the play, watching the wily producers convince sweet little old ladies to put their money into a Broadway show. And while laughing at their antics, you secretly thought, *Hmmm, produce a Broadway show… That does sound like fun.*

In real life, do only big shots put up the money? Actually, no. According to a recent *New York Times* report, the Tony-winning show *The Gentlemen's Guide to Love and Murder* had 130 investors who put up between $25,000 and $850,000 each for a total of 7.5 million.

Of course you shouldn't bet the farm. In fact, you will need to meet certain net-worth requirements for risky investments. But if you can afford the chance of losing your money, the fun and satisfaction might just be worth it to you. Think about opening-night tickets, maybe a party or two…and if the show wins a Tony, you all get to crowd onto the stage!

How would you get started on the path to becoming a producer? Try starting small on the local level. Many plays are developed in smaller markets first before heading to Broadway. For example, the LBJ play *All The Way* came not from the

New York theater scene but from Ashland, Oregon's Shakespeare Festival.

You can keep up on Broadway news through the Broadway League trade association or Broadway.org, which announces previews. If you attend a preview and fall in love with the play and its prospects, you could always raise your hand and see if they still need money. A production can take in more investors up until opening night.

RESOURCES
www.broadway.org
www.broadwayleague.com/

Participate in Audubon's Annual Bird Count

The Audubon Society has organized nationwide bird counts in which thousands of bird lovers participate year after year. In the winter the society holds the Christmas Bird Count from December 14 to January 5. For Valentine's Day there is a Backyard Bird Count, and in the summer you can participate in hummingbird counts.

Why should you participate? Because citizen science matters, and if birds and nature are your thing, you should help with this important effort. You don't need special skills—just your ability to look out the window and count what you see. Sometimes the counts take place out in the field; sometimes you can do it from your living-room window by drawing an imaginary circle and noting the birds that land or fly through it.

For more than one hundred years, Audubon has been holding the Christmas Bird Count. It is acknowledged to be the largest and longest-running citizen science effort in the world. Shouldn't you be doing it too?

> **RESOURCES**
> www.audubon.org/birds
> www.audubon.org/conservation/science/christmas-bird-count

Run for Office

Our forefathers envisioned a country in which ordinary citizens would periodically serve in office for a short time, not one in which a handful of professional politicians would cycle through office after office for decades at a time. So, maybe it is your turn to step up and serve. It would be naive to imagine that

Every state governor and most town mayors have a lengthy list of boards and commissions to which they need to appoint citizens. Is there a commission that suits your interest and skills? If so, speak up. Ask to be appointed. College student Julian Sander raised his hand for Nevada Governor Brian Sandoval's Business Roundtable on Education. "I figured who better to represent the student population." He'd heard about the new board on the radio and sent the governor an email describing how he could add to the discussion.

you could declare your candidacy, make a few signs, attend a few meetings, and mount a successful run for a statewide office, but many local offices still depend on the active participation of ordinary townsfolk. These may include school boards, city councils, fire districts, water boards, and other branches of local government.

Ellen Brazil Hasness worked in Washington, DC, for years and had a bird's-eye view of national politics and politicians. After retirement, she and her husband spent several years sailing around the Caribbean before reestablishing themselves in a small town in her native state. And it wasn't long before she felt the urge to get involved in local politics. "I figure if I can sail the ocean blue, I can do this," she said. Ellen won her race and now can pursue her bucket list goal to "take our little town into the future."

So, does your town—big or little—need you to do to help it into the future? Think about it... And who knows? You might start small and local and then feel the need to move up into another office in which you could have an even larger impact.

RESOURCES

The Campaign Manager: Running and Winning Local Elections (Catherine Shaw, Westview Press, 2014)

"In wisdom gathered over time I have found that every experience is a form of exploration."
—ANSEL ADAMS

Start a Humanitarian Movement

Famed San Francisco socialite Pat Montandon decided during the Reagan administration that something was more important than parties—world peace. She turned her attention to creating a group called Children as Teachers of Peace and gathered groups of young children to tour the world, calling on world leaders and delivering messages of hope and cooperation. They unfurled a handmade peace banner on the Great Wall of China, met with the leader of the Soviet Union, and had an audience with the Pope. Did she have a background in creating nonprofits and organizing? No. She simply had a passion and the means to pursue it.

We are all global citizens, and the answers to the world's problems may lie more with ordinary folks rising up and trying to make change than with our leaders. Is there a world problem you feel passionate about?

Grandmothers for Peace was founded in 1981 by a grandmother, Barbara Wiedner, who grew alarmed at the proliferation of nuclear weapons. She believed that "the world is safer in grandmas' arms." Out of her own personal protest, she began to organize others and soon enough an organization was created.

Do you have humanitarian stirrings? No doubt many others share your views. You could start small with a discussion group in your home with like-minded people, or begin to encourage change through a letter-writing campaign.

Big movements grow from small beginnings. They always have. Start small and watch your humanitarian movement grow.

"One of the inescapable encumbrances of leading an interesting life is that there have to be moments when you almost lose it."
—**JIMMY BUFFETT**

Participate in Cutting-Edge Scientific Research

Science and medicine are advanced through experimentation. And experiments need subjects, most often volunteers. Is it time for you to raise your hand and become a research participant? Rather than waiting until a medical condition arises and then requesting an experimental drug, you could be helping now by being the healthy participant. Volunteers are an integral part of the research process, and without a steady stream of volunteers, studies wouldn't be possible.

"My two young sons were involved in a scientific study at a local research university to try to find the cause of autism," says Beanie Bern. "They needed nonautistic boys to study, and I loved the idea that they could help. And they felt very important too. Years from now I hope they can claim to have played a small role in discovering more about autism."

Check the website of a research hospital near you, or visit the websites listed here to see what trials are actively seeking volunteers. Wouldn't it be great if you helped cure cancer?

RESOURCES

www.researchmatch.org

www.clinicaltrials.gov

Get Ready to Be a Hero

Sign up for a CPR class? Seriously? This seems so ordinary, somewhat mundane, and so very mature and sensible. How can this be a bucket list item? Because it should be. What greater honor and accomplishment is there than to save the life of another person?

For CPR a four-hour class is standard, and you can find one near you through the Red Cross website. You also can take free online courses at your own pace to understand the basic moves. The theory behind CPR has changed over the years and now focuses more on chest compressions and less on rescue breathing. The recommended pace to compress is to the beat of the Bee Gees' "Stayin' Alive."

If you're still not convinced the training is worth it, consider this: learning CPR and other lifesaving techniques is downright practical. Automated external defibrillator (AED) paddles now hang in some office buildings and airports, but would you know how to use them in an emergency? Learning to properly operate AEDs is another skill available through the Red Cross.

In an emergency, you don't want to be standing around uncertain of what to do. You need to acquire the skills and gain the confidence to respond. You might save your partner's life, your grandchild's, a neighbor's, or a total stranger's. And you will know what to do.

RESOURCES
www.redcross.org

Are you devoted to your big dog? Maybe your dog could train to save lives too. Big breeds like German shepherds and Labs make great search-and-rescue dogs, and training your dog to do that could bring you into a whole new world of activity and travel. Important work. You can find information on how to begin training at www.disasterdog.org.

Focus on Family

Fancy trips, expensive dinners, wonderful artwork, and passionate friends all make for a well-lived life. But if any of these things come at the expense of building a close and loving relationship with our own family, what have we really achieved? So many items on a bucket list cost money, but the lasting warmth and sense of accomplishment from building a close family unit are not only free but priceless. If you don't already have this in your life, is it time to refocus the list and move this item to the very top?

Page after page of this bucket list book contains ideas and opportunities that could be put to use as a way to draw your family closer. Is there a way to involve the people around you as you work to achieve your dreams? Siblings, partners, spouses, children, grandchildren, cousins… No matter which of the ideas you decide to pursue, extend the invitation for them to join you in the journey.

Maybe your son would jump at the chance to learn Spanish with you. Your granddaughter might enjoy attending a meeting of a classic car group. Your spouse might step forward and help you start a grassroots neighborhood group to clean up graffiti. A cousin might be longing to journal and will join you in your new vow to write every day for at least ten minutes.

Look around you. Who else wants to come along on the adventure of a lifetime? You may be surprised at who steps forward.

.... ✳ ....

OFF THE BEATEN PATH:
One-of-a-Kind Travel Experiences

GREAT WAYS TO GET THERE

Leaving on a (Private) Jet Plane

Is private jet travel on your bucket list? Most of the time, it's an extremely expensive undertaking, but there are several less-expensive ways to take a ride and experience that exclusive thrill. The best way, of course, is to have a friend with a plane. If you have a friend who does (or who knows how to fly), ask if they'd let you ride along sometime. Of course, etiquette rules apply when you are given the opportunity to catch a ride on a friend's plane: *always* be on time. Wheels up is wheels up, so do not make them

THE BIG BUCKET LIST BOOK

Are you headed somewhere with a large group of friends? Perhaps you can all charter a plane together. On my way to a friend's birthday bash in Baja, we and thirteen other party guests rented a plane to fly us from the Cabo San Lucas airport to the resort along the coast. It was less than two hundred dollars per person, and we got to skip the three-hour van ride usually required for this destination.

wait for you, because they won't. Also, you can't bring your dog or pets unless they tell you it is okay, and ask in advance about how much luggage you can bring.

But if you don't have a friend with a plane, then what? Check out the JetSuite website. By signing up to get alerts on last-minute bargains, you might find something that works for you. "Suitedeals" can be had for as little as $550 one way for the *whole* four-person plane. Imagine... You could bring three of your friends or your family—or have the whole jet to yourself! Note that these deals are often on specific routes, mostly when jets are being moved from one place to another according to someone else's needs. Check the website every so often until you find something that works near you, and jump on with some of your friends.

RESOURCES

www.jetsuite.com

Ride in a Vintage Bike Race in Tuscany

Yes, one of those organized bike rides through a beautiful part of the countryside has long been a dream of yours, hasn't it? Ride a little, eat a little, drink a little, sleep in a charming and rustic inn, that sort of thing. In France, maybe. Or Italy.

That's nice, but why not take it a step further and make it really unique? First, imagine biking in a group on white gravel roads through Tuscany. Now imagine that everyone around you, as far as the eye could see, is dressed in vintage cycling clothes and riding on classic bicycles. Now *that* would be cool. And it is real: it's a large race called the Eroica. Held every year on the first Sunday of October (a lovely time to cycle through the countryside anywhere!) in the Italian town of Gaiole, it is styled after a bygone era. This is not a bike race filled with spandex and high-tech cycling. These riders take the throwback idea seriously and are often dressed in old-time clothes and riding astride single-gear bikes from decades ago.

A local man started the race because he wanted to help preserve the famed white gravel roads in his region. The race started with fewer than a hundred vintage riders and has grown to a crowd of several thousand.

Don't have a vintage bike and a suitable outfit you can ship over to Italy for the race? Not to worry. You can rent appropriate bikes, and there is a large open-air market where all manner of classic and vintage apparel is sold.

But maybe you'd prefer to skip the throngs of other bicyclists and do it yourself, riding along the gravel roads at a slower pace. The English travel company Discovery Travel offers a self-guided 108-mile trip through the same region. Their package includes a twenty-one-gear bike, which might help you navigate those "undulating hills" easier than the old single-speed cruiser would.

RESOURCES

www.eroicagaiole.com

www.discoverytravel.co.uk/trips/strade-bianchi-white-roads-of-tuscany/

www.steel-vintage.com

See the World on Horseback

Perhaps you longed for a horse as a child, but never had enough chances to ride. Never fear, you can still indulge that childhood longing by seeking out trips on horseback. From dude ranches like the Turpin Meadow Ranch outside Jackson Hole, Wyoming, which will happily arrange a horse trekking trip into the Grand Tetons, to riding horseback on beaches in Aruba and in exotic locals like India, where you can travel on a rare breed of Marwari horse from palace to palace, there are ample opportunities to sit astride and see the world from another angle.

Equitours specializes in these trips. On their website you will find everything from a stay in a Tuscan villa to tours of ancient ruins and rain-forest adventures in Costa Rica.

RESOURCES

www.equitours.com

www.turpinmeadowranch.com

Make a Pilgrimage in Spain

Life really *is* a journey, and the best way to remember that our time on earth isn't just about goals accomplished or tasks ticked off is to make a pilgrimage. One of the most famous is the centuries–old 450-mile Camino de Santiago in Spain. Set aside a month for the basic trek and another six to seven days to savor the beauty along the way. Wearing good boots and carrying the basics—clothing, rain gear, and water—you'll journey through rustic villages, across dusty plains, and though challenging mountain passes with companions from around the world.

Anne Basye and her former college roommate Janet Murray walked a few years back. Anne describes it this way:

> For thirty days your rhythm will be predictable. After a café con leche and a roll, you'll walk a few miles with fellow pilgrims and share a picnic lunch by the side of the road. Some miles later (ten to twelve a day, typically), you'll check into your hostel or albergue by 4:00 p.m., shower and rinse out your socks, change your clothes, and tuck into an early ten-pilgrim dinner replete with a bottle of local wine. By eight thirty or nine you'll be on your bunk bed in a dorm filled with dozens more pilgrims gathering strength to do the same thing again tomorrow.

Just like life, Anne says the journey will "mix the unforgettable (meals, sunsets, vistas, conversations) with the mundane and the painful (blisters, sunburns, rain showers, bug bites). And when you reach

Santiago—one of the world's most beautiful cities, by the way—you'll be so enamored of life on the road that you'll want to keep going." Visit the informative American Pilgrims website hosted by North Americans who have walked the way.

In North America, a pilgrim path is growing and developing at El Santuario de Chimayo in New Mexico, and grants are in the works to develop a similar pilgrim path among the California missions.

> **RESOURCES**
> www.elcaminosantiago.com
> www.americanpilgrims.com/
> www.elsantuariodechimayo.us/Santuario/
> GuidanceOnPilgrimages.html

Learn How to Use All Four Wheels at the Overland Expo

Live in the city but own a four-wheel-drive vehicle? Wish you had a chance to give it a bit of free rein off road? Lie awake at night imagining what it would be like to chuck it all, toss a sleeping bag and a guitar in the back, and start driving to Peru? Plenty of folks do just that, and you can meet them all and learn at the twice-annual Overland Expo. Held in Arizona and North Carolina, the Expo offers more than a hundred classes and seminars, including how to navigate (GPS doesn't work in the outback, now does it?) and cook simple dishes outdoors on the road. A bushcraft area focuses on wilderness survival tips and primitive technology you can build and use on the road, should you need it.

Take the Land Rover overland driving course to hone your skills, using your own vehicle or the test vehicle. The Expo also offers motorcycle skills courses staffed by BMW and activities at the Adventure Motorcycle Rodeo Arena.

RESOURCES
www.overlandexpo.com

Cross the Seas in an Ocean Liner

The idea of ship travel holds great allure and romance, but being aboard an enormous floating suburban mall of a cruise ship doesn't appeal to everyone. The idea of an ocean crossing in a large ship with just a handful of other passengers retains much of the glamour of yesteryear.

My parents, George and Mary Alice Basye, sailed the West Coast in 1981 on an American President Lines container ship headed with a load to Egypt, which they were hoping to see for a little while before the ship returned to the United States. Alas, just as they arrived, Egyptian President Anwar Sadat was assassinated and the country was in turmoil. Rather than wait for another load, the ship turned around and came back empty, making for one bumpy ride across the Atlantic, which wasn't part of my parents' plan! But they had to do it or risk being stranded there. Traveling on freighters, you must always remember that these are working ships, not passenger ships, and that their priority is to haul freight.

Traveling onboard a working freighter is an opportunity only for the very seasoned traveler. Rather than having the posh and glamorous layout of a cruise ship, a working freighter has only a few staterooms and so only a few passengers. Ships carrying more than a certain number of passengers are required to have a doctor onboard, and freighters do not. However, you will dine often with the captain and sometimes the radio man.

If this doesn't intimidate you, check the Freighter Cruises website for where the ships go and how much the voyages cost. Far less than a cruise, of course, but remember you are on a working ship whose sole focus is getting their cargo to port on time. You will have done something that few other folks have the nerve to do though. How does this sound for a route: Houston to New Orleans to the Bahamas to Portugal to Spain to several ports in Italy before heading back to Spain, Portugal, and the Bahamas, adding Florida and two ports of call in Mexico before heading back to Houston. Every seven weeks that is the route of the *Buxcliff*. Pack a suitcase full of books to read, and settle in for the long haul.

> ### RESOURCES
>
> www.freightercruises.com
>
> www.freighter-travel.com
>
> www.cruisepeople.co.uk

Old Roads, New Experiences

The Unites States has several well-known and well-traveled original highways. In the West you'll find Route 66, Highway 40, and Highway 1. Back East, some people get dreamy looks thinking of driving U.S. 1, the elevated road that links the Florida Keys. You can drive from island to island, from Key Largo to Key West, all the time marveling at the amount of construction and engineering that was involved in building the road.

The Pacific Coast Highway in California stretches the length of the state through different types of regions and communities—from the laid-back surf towns like Dana Point all the way up to the thickly forested areas around Eureka. Which old road do you dream of driving?

Peter Sander, an Ohio native and longtime road tripper, filled us in on some of the choices.

The most famous route of all is the heralded Route 66 from Chicago to Los Angeles, also known as "Main Street of America" or the "Will Rogers Highway"—but this route has largely been superseded by interstates and formally ceased to exist in 1985. A few chunks of the old road remain in parallel to Interstate 40 in Arizona, but for the most part this road and its tantalizing historic travel infrastructure are gone.

Instead of Route 66, try one of the country's many long stretches of lonely road, some literally in the middle of nowhere, some running more or less parallel to existing interstates. All provide a great glimpse into the travel experience of the past and are a fun ride. U.S. 50 still runs across the country from Sacramento, California, to Ocean City, Maryland. The most interesting stretch—between Carson City, Nevada and Salina, Utah—is aptly named "The Loneliest Road in America." It passes through stunning Great Basin desertscapes and old mining camps with intriguing names like Eureka, Nevada. Also not to be missed is America's newest and least visited national park, Great Basin National Park, outside Ely, Nevada.

A fun ride can also be had on U.S. 6, the "Grand Army of the Republic Highway," which starts out in Bishop, California, east of the Sierra Nevada range, heads east through another more southerly chunk of the Nevada desert and Soldier Summit in Utah, runs parallel to several interstate highways but in many places takes a route of its own, finally ending up (or starting out, depending on which way you're going) on the tip of Cape Cod. Along the way are many scenic and cultural tastes of a past-tense America, including the communal Amish-like Amana Colonies in east central Iowa.

Interesting rides can also be found on desolate U.S. 2, running from Michigan's Upper Peninsula west to Everett, Washington, largely just south of the United

States and Canada's border. Not surprisingly, it's been called "America's Air-Conditioned Highway" and passes through remote outposts like Havre (that's pronounced Have-er), Montana, and the Teddy Roosevelt National Park in northern North Dakota. U.S. 30 parallels the original Union Pacific Railroad alignment through central Nebraska— plenty of grain elevators and A&W root beer stands along this one—and 135 trains a day run along the busy mainline just to add a bit of interest.

- Highway 2: Everett, Washington, to St. Ignace, Michigan
- Interstate 5: Border to border, Mexico to Canada
- Highway 6: Bishop, California, to Provincetown, Massachusetts
- Highway 41: Miami, Florida, to Copper Harbor, Michigan
- Highway 50: Sacramento, California, to Ocean City, Maryland
- Highway 287: Choteau, Montana, to Port Arthur, Texas

If you're headed north or south, there's always U.S. 41 of Allman Brothers "Ramblin' Man" fame, and U.S. 287 from Canada to Mexico along the eastern slopes of the Rockies. Anywhere you go, you'll get a different travel experience, laced with images of the past and largely devoid of the big trucks and gotta-get-there drivers found on most of today's major highways.

Hike the Trails of the World, from California to the Alps

The book *Wild* spawned a thousand solo women backpackers on the Pacific Crest Trail, which is one long and dusty road. Not all of us are cut out to hoist on a heavy pack and spend weeks or months on the trail's segments from Mexico to Canada. What can the rest of us do? How about shorter hikes from hut to hut? Hut-to-hut hiking could be the way to go.

Longtime friends Laura Lynne Powell and Jasmin Hakes didn't have time for the entire Pacific Crest Trail, so they focused on a part where they could start out from a rustic lodge and hike back at the end of the day, knowing that a glass of wine awaited them. "We started hiking at dawn right outside our door," Laura Lynne said, "and felt transformed by every step and every second as the sun rose on the horizon, changing the landscape around us. It was a natural high!"

In Colorado, an entire system of huts was developed during World War II for troop-training purposes. When the war ended, the 10th Mountain Division huts became civilian hiking destinations. There are thirty-four back-country huts altogether, some easier to get to than others.

While Colorado has thirty-four, the Alps have some three thousand huts scattered through several countries.

You can find the German Alps hut information on the Germany Is Wunderbar website.

Another hiking trail to dip in and out of is the Appalachian Trail, one of the world's longest continuously marked trails. It's more than 2,000 miles long, wandering through fourteen states, and visited by several million people a year. Not all at once, thankfully. Although some sturdy souls set out to hike the entire length, far more choose smaller sections to suit their own schedule. The Appalachian Trail Conservancy site is filled with information on which parts of the trail are easy and which parts are strenuous, as well as what times of the year are best to catch the fall colors along the way.

Finally going on a long-awaited journey or to a long-anticipated event? Why not prolong the experience by walking there? A few years back an enterprising young man decided that he would walk to the World Cup—through all of South America! That might be considered a tad extreme, but what a great way to steep yourself in an experience that otherwise might pass by quickly!

Perhaps you could walk the same route you drive every day, just to see what the experience is like on the ground. Literally. It might open your eyes to seeing your community in a whole new light.

Don't feel that you're not a real hiker unless you're hauling a pack and spending months on the dirt trail. Get out there and do as much or as little as suits you. It's all good.

Drive a Boat down the Canals of France and Germany

You've seen pictures of the elegant, narrow boats navigating a French canal, and you can envision yourself onboard, wineglass in hand, as the scenery floats by. What are you waiting for? The company LeBoat will not only rent you a lovely little boat but actually teach you what you need to know to operate the boat yourself and then send you on your way. They operate in several countries, in case you have a wide array of fantasies to fulfill. The Canal du Midi in the South of France? Down the Thames in England? Motor toward Trieste? Float past medieval timber houses in Germany? Yes, all of those are possible.

Though be forewarned: you probably want to have some basic boating experience or get a couple lessons before you go. While LeBoat offers basic tutorials, they may not be sufficient for longer or more complicated excursions or itineraries. Publishing executive Stephanie Bowen and her family almost found themselves in over their heads (thankfully not literally!) when they rented a canal boat from LeBoat for two weeks without prior experience sailing or driving a boat. But they quickly caught on, and she said it was truly the experience of a lifetime (and she even learned a new skill while she was at it).

In Northern France you will find Catherine Saint-James and her charming two-boat company Ille Flottante. You can float through Brittany in brand-new custom boats that look like small gypsy caravans and sleep two. The website is in French, but just send her an email and she can respond in English.

What about living on a houseboat in Paris? You know you want to. The *Viking* is tied up on the Seine near the Bois de Boulogne, about ten minutes from the center of town. The boat is usually rented out for long stretches and therefore unavailable, but it's well worth checking to see if it is available.

◆ www.parishouseboat.com

RESOURCES

www.leboat.com

www.illeflottante.com

Ever gone somewhere new, found a unique local item, and thought, "Gee, maybe I should try to import these…"? Karen Shuppert went to San Miguel de Allende for a visit and came home with a business. "I bought a pair of shoes at a local store, and once I was back in the States, total strangers would stop me to ask about them. Even men, and they never want to talk about shoes!" Karen went back to San Miguel de Allende and approached the family that manufactures the shoes, and an international business was born.

HISTORIC AND LITERARY DESTINATIONS

Stay at an Actual Artists' Colony

We all have preconceived notions of what an artists' colony should be like, and then we get there and…eh, chances are we're disappointed by what we find. It seems a bit like what we already have at home, over in the mall. Buck up and try again, this time in Mexico. San Miguel de Allende is the real thing. Cobblestone streets, charming houses hidden behind doors and courtyard gates, art and artists everywhere. This is not your touristy kitsch; this is serious Mexican art. Although there has been a strong American expat and retiree scene here for many decades, the local Mexican culture is readily apparent and has not disappeared underneath the other influences.

Frequent visitors to San Miguel de Allende like its feeling of safety and the fact that it is filled with folks who are not there to party. Because it is not a coastal resort like Mazatlan or Ixtapa, there is no spring-break or college-student party scene. Another plus is that there are several interesting small towns nearby for easy day trips. In 2008, UNESCO declared the town a Cultural Heritage for Humanity site.

RESOURCES

www.sanmiguel-de-allende.com

Forget African Safaris. Try an Indian Safari!

An African safari experience is a fairly common aspiration for many international travelers. Why be like all of your friends though? Why not go to India on safari? And watch leopards in the wild.

The Jawai leopard camp opened in 2013 and quickly made its way to the top of travel magazine lists of the world's best hotels. Small and, needless to say, luxurious, the camp has only ten tents to suit the needs of visitors. Accessible from Udaipur, a major destination, the region boasts an entirely different landscape than the rest of Rajasthan. This is one place

Been longing to visit a far-flung place but reading the international news with growing dread? Act now. We live in a world that has always been unstable, and shifting political alliances can change the travel scene in an instant. Places that were once high on everyone's list are suddenly under siege and no longer standard travel destinations. I'm not sure I will get to go to Egypt anytime soon, and a planned trip to Turkey in a few years time might well crumble. Jump on a plane now or forever regret not taking the chance.

that will trump anyplace your friends think they can brag about. Check out the Sujan Luxury website.

Sri Lanka is another unusual safari destination. From the Sinharaja rain forest to Bundala National Park, this fascinating country offers a range of terrains and wildlife experiences. Leopards are found here too, as are sloths, elephants, mongoose, and more.

RESOURCES

www.sujanluxury.com

www.srilankansafari.com

Attend a Masked Ball in Venice

Does it get any more dreamily romantic than this—the idea of attending one of the many masked balls that take place in Venice during the winter Carnival season? It sounds unattainable, like the masked balls would be strictly for European royalty, but in fact they have a long tradition of being open to the paying public. Not only can you buy a ticket to some of the most exclusive ones, like Il Ballo del Doge, but you can also rent incredible ball gowns and men's costumes to wear to the event.

The Venice Carnival Italy website has details on the balls and ticket prices, which range from around five hundred euros to attend the late-evening, dance-only portion of a ball to several thousand euros for a ticket that includes a reception, a dinner, and dancing far into the night. Costumes are in a similar range—from simple, modestly priced rentals to extravagant, over-the-top outfits for many hundreds of euros. Antonia Sautter, an Italian period costume designer, is the organizer of many of the masked balls and rents costumes to many of the attendees.

RESOURCES

www.venice-carnival-italy.com

Explore the Literary South

For lovers of literature, Oxford, Mississippi, is a famed destination. Plan a trip of several days, check into a comfy spot, and settle in to soak up the atmosphere.

Faulkner was here, nearby in his famed Rowan Oak home, now a popular tourist attraction. John Grisham lived in the area for many years, and National Book Award winner Jesmyn Ward has lived here, too. If you have a football fan who travels with you, you might drop the news that Eli Manning lives in Oxford during the off-season.

In addition to the aura of authors nearby, Oxford boasts what *Publishers Weekly* recently named the "Bookstore of the Year." Square Books was founded in 1979 and has grown into a three-store complex on the courthouse square that's a constant hub of activity. Check their website to see what authors are appearing. It is a well-known stop on many book publicity tours for big-name authors.

Where else can you go? Fairhope, Alabama, and you might run into Winston Groom of *Forrest Gump* fame. Harper Lee's new novel, published more than fifty years after the release of *To Kill a Mockingbird*, will send lit fans on renewed pilgrimages to her hometown of Monroeville, Alabama. Tennessee Williams, Truman Capote, and Anne Rice are long gone from New Orleans, but you can still commune with their presence over a Sazarac cocktail or two.

RESOURCES

A Visitor's Guide to the Literary South (Trish Foxwell, Countryman Press, 2013)

Tour Literary and Book Towns

The ultimate book lover's destination is the Welsh town of Hay on Wye. On the border with England, this quaint town is totally devoted to books— antiquarian books, collectible books, out-of-print, you name it. Whether collecting, selling, or reading, here you can freely indulge in your passion. For almost thirty years, Hay on Wye has held a book festival in late May, but other literary and cultural events are scattered throughout the year.

Closer to home, you will find a book town in Archer City, Texas. It was created by bestselling author Larry McMurtry of *Lonesome Dove* fame, who has long been a book dealer in addition to his writing career. His store Booked Up carries between 150,000 and 200,000 fine and scholarly books. In past years he had as many as four different buildings in Archer City devoted to his stock, but in 2012 he held a huge auction to sell off a few hundred thousand (seriously) volumes and scale down to just the one location. Visit the Booked Up website for more information.

"Customers come to us from wherever the four winds blow," McMurtry says about his customer base. Perhaps you too will blow that way soon.

RESOURCES

www.hayfestival.com

www.bookedupac.com

Travel Iceland's Ring Road of Fire and Ice

Writer and publisher Kim Wyatt has lived in many of the places on other people's bucket lists—Yosemite National Park, Alaska, Japan, and now Lake Tahoe. Is there another place that draws her now? Yes, Iceland is next on the list.

A few years ago, a psychic told me unsolicited and with urgency that I must go to Iceland. Apparently, I came from there in a past life and, along with my family, lived in the dirt and sod before civilization. The psychic could see me and my father side-by-side, digging in the dirt. (This struck a nerve, because we do forage for mushrooms together, often side-by-side in the dirt.)

When I made it to Iceland, the psychic told me, all in life would be revealed. Everything that had come before would make sense, and my direction from that point on would be seamless and charmed. In fact, if I wanted this to be my last lifetime, I could make it so. Self-actualization or nirvana is within my reach, she said. I just need to get to Iceland.

A tall order. What would one do once the plane landed? Iceland sometimes sounds like, well, just ice. But it is now firmly on Kim's bucket list.

"I plan to travel the Ring Road, a sequence of fire and ice that circles the island. I will rent a camper van and take my time covering 828 miles. Fjords, waterfalls, beaches, glaciers, hot springs, lakes, caves, volcanoes, northern lights, whales, and reindeer. The Library of Water, Björk, feminism. Reading this list, I almost

Tired of hanging around airports on uncomfortable seats during flight delays but not a member of any airline clubs where you can hide out? Many airport lounges in airports grant access for a onetime fee. Download the Lounge Buddy app (www .loungebuddy.com) and never be stuck again. And why not up your rock-star status by every so often splurging and taking a limo to the airport, shipping your luggage ahead instead of dragging it with you, and having the hotel concierge on the other end already working to book your dinner reservations before you leave home.

believe I will be coming home." When to visit? Oddly winter can be one of the best times, as the temperature there can be warmer than in New York or London or Paris. And there are always hot springs to warm you up.

RESOURCES
www.iceland.is

Walk in Our Leaders' Footsteps: Visit Presidential Homes

There are many wonderful driving trips in the United States, but what could be more quintessentially American than an extended vacation to visit the homes of several presidents? From Mount Vernon to Monticello, Harry Truman's home in Independence, Missouri, or his Little White House in Key West, to Andrew Jackson's Hermitage outside Nashville, and several points in between, you could easily spend the summer on the road discovering more about the presidents and our country at the same time. Make sure you include President Lincoln's Cottage just outside Washington, DC, where Abraham Lincoln retreated regularly during the Civil War. He wrote the Emancipation Proclamation during one of his stays there. Guided tours are given on most non-holiday days.

Pop in the audio versions of presidential biographies like *Washington: A Life* by Ron Chernow or *American Lion: Andrew Jackson in the White House* by Jon Meacham while you drive to enhance your understanding of the man and his world once you arrive.

RESOURCES

www.monticello.org

www.nps.gov

www.trumanlittlewhitehouse.com

www.thehermitage.com

www.lincolncottage.org

Join Dylan Thomas's Birthday Walk

The poet Dylan Thomas turned one hundred in 2014, except that he actually died when he was thirty-nine. His poem, "On His Birthday," begins, "In the mustardseed sun, by full tilt river and switch-back sea," and goes on to describe a walk Thomas took on his thirty-fifth birthday. This is a walk that you can take too.

Whether or not it is your actual birthday, the Welsh town of Laugharne would love to have you visit and walk this same path. A local farmer who had made it a custom to recite the poem on the spot on his own birthday successfully lobbied the town to create the Dylan Thomas Birthday Walk. Farmer Bob Stevens cleared the view to achieve more of what Thomas would have seen decades ago by trimming trees, and the town added benches and plaques along the route.

Wouldn't this be a fine and literary way to mark an important birthday in your own life? A local pub where Dylan Thomas liked to drink will even give you a break on the price of a drink if you arrive on your own birthday.

RESOURCES
www.dylanthomasbirthdaywalk.co.uk

See an Opera under the Stars

Summer opera festivals abound. No need to dress up and drape yourself with finery if you are throwing on a sweater and packing a heavy blanket to sit under the stars at some of these venues around the world. How many can you visit?

Among the best-known summer festivals are Santa Fe, New Mexico; Ravinia outside of Chicago; and Chautauqua Opera in New York. You could criss-cross the country all summer long before heading out internationally to take in outdoor festivals all over Italy, Hungary, and the UK, or attend the famous festival devoted to the works of Richard Wagner at Bayreuth, Germany. Although most are fairly casual affairs, the Glyndebourne Opera Festival outside London is quite a bit dressier.

Even if you don't start off as much of an opera fan, by the time you have finished picnicking in all of these lovely places you might find yourself humming along. Many major opera and symphony companies also give free outdoor performances in the summer. The Metropolitan Opera draws a crowd of many thousands to the lawn in Central Park for their summer offerings, and San Francisco Opera holds theirs in a baseball stadium. It's another way to get a double dose of sunshine and culture.

RESOURCES

www.metopera.org

www.sfopera.com

www.santafeopera.org

www.ravinia.org

www.glyndebourne.com

www.bayreuther-festspiele.de/english/english_156.html

Rekindle Memories down by the Sea

Do you have fond memories of a childhood vacation with the entire family, maybe a camping trip deep in the woods where you first heard a spooky campfire story, or a long, meandering walk on the beach to search for sea glass with your mother? And you haven't been back to the spot since… So why not now?

Karen Phillips gathered her family members as an adult and invited them all to join her at the place they used to go when they were small. "This time you can stay up as late as you want!" she enthused. "You can buy those earrings in the gift shop. You won't have to sneak a beer or a smoke behind the garage. You are an adult. Do what you want in the place you were a child."

Why not try to gather your own clan for a visit to an old family vacation spot? Is the same old hotel still there? That funny old diner with the really great hot dogs? You'll never know how much of your childhood memory still exists until you go looking for it.

Re-create a beloved vacation, or try to reassemble and heal from one that went horribly wrong! You have a chance to make it work this time.

If you can re-create a beloved childhood vacation, should you take your own children? Maybe, but then again maybe not. They might cramp your style the same way your parents did so many years ago!

Dip Your Toes into a Piece of History—Literally: Visit One of the World's Top Pools

Are you a swimmer who likes to move back and forth through shimmering blue liquid, lap after lap? Or perhaps you'd prefer poolside lounging and raising a languid hand every so often in the direction of someone who could freshen your drink. No matter what your watery focus is, drawing up a list of pools around the world in which to dip your toes some day is a pleasant task. Here are a few ideas to get you started swimming in luxury.

How about dipping into the much-photographed Neptune or Roman Pools at California's famed Hearst Castle? Not out of the question if you have donated enough to the Friends of Hearst Castle foundation.

But famous pools connected to hotels are available

to guests and thus easier to get wet in. Johnny
Weissmuller frequented the Biltmore in Coral Gables,
Florida, before he gained fame as Tarzan—when he
was a mere Olympian. On the West Coast, San Diego
boasts the Weissmuller Pool at the Lafayette Hotel
and Swim Club. Up the road from there in Santa
Monica you can swim in the pool built for William
Randolph Hearst's longtime mistress Marion Davies
for far less than donating enough to swim at Hearst
Castle. Davies's former beachside pool opened to the
public a few years back, so lounging beside it is perfectly affordable.

Swimming farther afield will take you to cliff-
side pools on the Mediterranean like the 1920s Le
Corbusier-designed Punta Tragara in Capri or the
Hôtel du Cap-Eden-Roc in Cannes.

Hungary and Germany also have a famous pool or
two. "It looks like you are walking into the 1930s,"
says Roxanne Langer of the famous pool at the Hotel
Gellért in Budapest. "You feel like a movie star. And
if you want to look like a movie star after all the
Hungarian pastries you will need to jump in and start
swimming laps!" In Berlin the Badeschiff is a floating
river barge with a pool that is open to the elements
in the summer and under a big protective bubble the

rest of the year. Intrigued? Let the waters be your guide as you plan one long swim into the future…

RESOURCES

www.friendsofhearstcastle.org

www.biltmorehotel.com

www.lafayettehotelsd.com

www.beachhouse.smgov.net

www.hoteltragara.com

www.hotel-du-cap-eden-roc.com

www.gellertbath.com

www.slowtravelberlin.com/the-badeschiff/

Learn How to Survive in the Wild

You've seen him often enough on television, that English guy who gets dropped into deserts and such and tries to survive with just a knife and his wits. Bear Grylls. With a name like that, could he do anything else? And have you ever wondered, hmmm, how would I do alone in the mountains for a few days…

Bear Grylls can teach you what he knows, so that if that ever happened, you'd stand a much better chance of making it out alive. He runs a "survival academy" that holds classes in the UK, on both coasts in the United States, and for those who really want to go for it, in Africa. No need to pack a bag with various tools, because the camp loans them to you for the duration. And if you pass at the end, you will be presented with your very own Bear Grylls custom knife. Sounds like you really will have earned it!

Outward Bound also offers courses that teach outdoor survival skills, such as winter navigation and avalanche survival.

RESOURCES
www.beargryllssurvivalacademy.com
www.outwardbound.org

Experience Autumn on the Road

"Get together in October? No, I'm afraid we are always on the road in the fall…" Wouldn't that be nice to be able to say? Now, I understand that many people cannot get away in the fall or don't have much flexibility in when they can travel. But once your time is your own and you are permanently detached from the scheduling of office, school, and social activities in your hometown, try to schedule your major trips in the fall months. Why? Because fall is simply the best time of year to go anywhere you've been longing to go. The island of Capri is at its most peaceful. The Napa Valley hums with the sounds of harvest. The Hamptons are affordable and deserted. And our national parks are perfect... Elk rut in Yellowstone, bugling noisily in the distance as you wander around.

Not to mention the fact that flights are less expensive than during high season and most places are far cheaper to visit. Make it your goal to be permanently out of town from September on...returning only in time to host Thanksgiving in a relaxed mood from your various travels.

Here are five places well worth visiting in autumn:

Paris in September, when city residents return (la rentrée) after being in vacation mode.

New York in September, when Central Park is beautiful and the opera and symphony are back in action.

Hawaii, when the kids have gone back to school and the hotel rates drop dramatically.

Venice, which is otherworldly in November when the tourists leave and the fog rolls in.

*Off-season food and wine festivals in places like the
Barbados, which hosts its Food & Wine and Rum
Festival in November. (www.foodwinerum.com)*

Once you grow accustomed to visiting in the off-season, you'll never again succumb to the urge to fight a crowd during a region's high season. Stand in line to enter a museum? Not you. You haven't done it in years.

Visit the World's Christmas Markets and Dickens Fairs

Are you a total Christmas lover? Anxious to decorate the house the minute the turkey is cleared from the table at Thanksgiving? Eyeing the fuzzy red sweater in the back of your closest and longing for the days to turn cool enough to don it?

Here is a bucket list item for you then, a tour of the world's great Christmas markets. The tradition of Christmas markets goes back to the Middle Ages in Europe. Munich's was first held in the year 1310. All over Northern Europe you will find the markets—from Vienna and Salzburg to Prague, and into France in Strasbourg and Lille. The Christmas

Markets website has information on the many markets throughout Germany.

In the States you will find a similar holiday spirit at the Dickens fairs. San Francisco holds the largest every weekend in December, and the Scattle area also offers one every year. What will you find at a Dickens-themed Christmas fair? "In addition to the Dickens characters, there are historical characters of the Victorian era like Queen Victoria and Prince Albert, and even some fictional characters like Sherlock Holmes and Father Christmas," says Jennifer Aldrich, who spends her holiday weekends in costume as a member of a Dickens Fair cast. Would you want to wear a costume and volunteer in the San Francisco one? Check out the section of the Dickens Fair website on getting involved. Or see if a town closer to you offers this holiday event.

RESOURCES

www.christmasmarkets.com

www.dickensfair.com

BEDDING DOWN

Private Lives

Much is being made in the media about trendy travelers who turn their backs on hotels and stay instead in private homes. There has always been a group that has been able to avoid hotels in major cities and stay in less expensive digs in some of the best parts of town. Who? Members of private social clubs, that's who.

Many clubs have reciprocal arrangements with other clubs across the country and around the globe, so you might be able to justify the membership price by thinking of it as a way to expand your travel options. Not all of these private clubs have hotel quarters, but those that do are very comfortable and sometimes quite luxurious.

Wait, isn't it hard to get into these clubs? Yes, some of them, but others are reaching out to new segments of the population (Women, gasp! Non-WASPs, gulp!) in an effort to continue to survive. Belonging to a club does have an old-fashioned, retro feel to it, but sometimes that is the hippest feeling of all.

For those who can't (or don't want to) join these clubs, never fear! Getting a room in a private home is easier than ever before thanks to sites like Airbnb and

VRBO. There is no guarantee that the Parisian who rents you her spare bedroom wants to get chummy over a croissant or that the Chicago-based stewardess who rents her condo knows where to get the best deep-dish pizza. As you start to communicate with potential hosts online you will get a sense of how willing they are to engage.

RESOURCES

www.airbnb.com

www.vrbo.com

Live in a Castle

Growing up with children's illustrated picture books and fairy tales, who of us *didn't* daydream about living in a castle? More recently, the Harry Potter films treated us all to the tantalizing vision of the enormous Hogwarts castle high on a hill with turrets aplenty. Sure, you can stay in castles all over Europe because many have been converted into small hotels and guesthouses. Ah, but what if you don't want (or can't afford) to pay for the privilege?

Good news—you won't have to. Two years ago Cathleen Swanson spent months living in chateaus, castles, and small palaces at no cost to her. How? She'd signed up to be a temporary caretaker. "I lived in Ireland for a month while the owners traveled. I spent several weeks in a beautiful old stone house in a small village in France while the owner was in England for an operation, and then I spent a month in a white palace on a hill in southern Spain, down the street from Julio Iglesias's house while the owners were at a film festival."

So is it all fun and games? Well, no. Most owners are looking for someone to take care of their pets and water the garden while they are gone. But it's still a spectacular experience. Here is part of a recent entry from one of the sites you can join to learn about these opportunities:

House sitter needed for Vienne Chateau. "We live in a beautiful post-Renaissance style castle in remarkably good condition, situated between Tours and Poitiers. Couple or family wanted for three weeks house sitting. We are looking for a couple who can be active in the garden…mainly raking leaves and closing the gate at night." Sounds like a reasonable trade for a stay in a castle. Could this be you?

Check out the opportunities around the world at the Trusted Sitters website. A year's membership is $95 and allows you to contact the house owners directly. Cathleen does point out one thing to keep in mind: "Most of the castles were in remote places that get pretty cold in the winter, and that is when the owners want to travel. A good place and time to work on a book, I suppose."

RESOURCES

www.trustedhousesitters.com

See the United States in a Silver Bullet

Airstream trailers! They are everywhere now, the gleaming symbols of a bygone era. You've seen them, the long aluminum bullet-shaped vintage trailers that are suddenly chic. Some are carefully restored vintage affairs, and others are the newer version, and all are coveted. But they are not inexpensive. Even if you found a screaming deal parked in someone's side yard and forgotten for decades, the amount to restore it would be a stunner. You can rent them, but the price tag is a shocker there too. If that's your choice, the Rent an Airstream website has rates and availability. The Airstream2Go site is another option.

But if all you want is the experience of sleeping inside an Airstream without the hassle of hitching it to a pickup truck, there are many more ways to explore.

Here are a few recommendations for places around the country where you can stay in an Airstream trailer:

The Shady Dell in Bisbee, Arizona, www.theshadydell.com

Kate's Lazy Desert Airstream Motel in Landers, California, www.lazymeadow.com/index.php?page=lazy-desert

Shooting Star RV Resort in Escalante, Utah, www.shootingstar-rvresort.com

And if you want to take your love of Airstreams to Europe, check out the BelRepayre Airstream and Retro Trailer Park near Mirepoix, France.

Once you are hooked on the silver bullets, you might want to earmark Airstreamclassifieds.com. They list trailers in a wide range of prices and maintain a chat board to help with handy info like what to do if you are locked out of your Airstream.

RESOURCES

www.rentanairstream.com

www.airstream2go.com

www.airstreameurope.com

Have a Literary Sleepover in a Famous Author's House

Wonderful as it is to fall asleep with a book, what if you could fall asleep *in* the book? Or at least in the place where the author wrote the book. Although we usually imagine colonial India when we think of Rudyard Kipling, he actually spent time living in Vermont. Naulakha, the large house he lived in near Brattleboro, is now owned by the Landmark Trust USA and is available to rent for $390–$450 a night. To sit at Kipling's desk and gaze out a window that he once looked out… How much closer can you get to being in the story?

Prolific romance and mystery author Nora Roberts owns the Inn BoonsBoro in Boonsboro, Maryland, where the rooms are named after famous romantic pairings, like Rhett and Scarlett. And fans of James Bond creator Ian Fleming can rent his house in Jamaica, where he would bang out each Bond book over the course of a winter. You can rent one room, but bring your friends because it is a five-bedroom house. That way you can split the cost. (The low-season rate for five bedrooms is $5,500 a night.) Hemingway fans can't spend the night in his Key West residence, but you can get married or have a special event there.

163

What about spending the night inside a bookstore? In Paris the famed bookstore Shakespeare and Company (not the original one owned by Sylvia Beach, but one that she gave her blessing to) has always had a policy of allowing up to four writers, so-called "tumbleweeds," to spend the night. Some stay for weeks.

RESOURCES

landmarktrustusa.org/properties/rudyard-kiplings-naulakha/

www.innboonsboro.com

www.theflemingvilla.com

www.hemingwayhome.com

www.shakespeareandcompany.com/51
/shakespeare-and-company/56/tumbleweeding

Talk to Strangers

Yes, your mother told you not to talk to strangers when you were young, but you are a grown-up now and it is time to chat up the locals. It's been shown that the most memorable trips and experiences are ones in which travelers have had real and meaningful interactions with locals, not just a chat with a pleasant seatmate who spoke their language. Remember that time you helped an Italian villager change a flat tire? Of course you do. Or the time someone took pity on you in a local farmers market and helped you choose the best vegetables? Ah, you think of it often…

So how can you make sure that these kinds of things happen often in your life? Time to expand your horizons. Particularly when traveling, plunge in and start talking. The world is full of interesting people you haven't met yet.

In addition to doing this in your hometown, you can establish international friendships from the comfort of your own home. For decades the organization Servas has helped create friendships between people all over the world. You will need to be interviewed by a local contact before you can join, but once a member, you will have the chance to travel from place to place around the globe with an already existing network of members who joined to meet people from other places. To form international friendships and have deeper travel experiences. And to foster world peace and understanding. And who doesn't want that?

RESOURCES
www.usservas.org

Room 16 at L'Hotel in Paris is where Oscar Wilde died so many years ago. I share a birthday and a profession with Mr. Wilde, so I have always felt a certain kinship. Arriving at the hotel a few years back I stammered out the sentence I'd constructed on the train in my schoolgirl French. "*Je voudrais voir le chambre d'morte d'monsieur Wilde.*" *Ah, non, pas possible.* It was already booked. But I stayed in Room 19 and would pause on the spiral staircase every time I passed the door of 16, resting my hand on the door frame and speaking very softly to Oscar. For details go to www.l-hotel.com

I've never stayed at the famous Raffles Hotel in Singapore, but I did have a drink there once. Likewise the Mandarin Oriental in Bangkok. Instead of shelling out the cost of a room at some of the world's most famous hotels, why not put on your best outfit, stroll through the lobby, and sit at the bar for a drink? Soak up the atmosphere for a fraction of the price. In New York you can admire the Maxfield Parrish murals at the St. Regis's King Cole bar or the famed drawings in Bemelmans Bar at the Carlyle. Atmosphere available for just the price of a martini. What could be better?

Stay in the Favorite Hotels of the Stars

Where did your idols spend their last moments on earth? A war hero, a literary giant, a creative genius? Why not make a pilgrimage to the site and stand on the spot or sleep in the room where the great ones breathed their last. Close your eyes and begin the conversation you've imagined having with them.

Tell them what their life and accomplishments have meant to yours. Because they are there, and yes, they are listening.

If you aren't looking to commune in your hero's final hours, what about seeking out the spots they frequented? The Lodge at Sun Valley for Hemingway (you can rent the room where he wrote *For Whom the Bell Tolls*); Winston Churchill's favorite painting spots in Câmara de Lobos, a small fishing village on the island of Madeira; or FDR's much-loved presidential yacht, the *Potomac*, now anchored at Oakland, California's Jack London Square (where you can find Heinold's First and Last Chance Bar, the bar where Jack did his homework as a young boy).

RESOURCES

www.sunvalley.com/lodging/sun-valley-lodge/

www.madeiraisland.com

www.usspotomac.org

www.heinolds.com

A Castle of One's Own

You can pay to stay in many castles and can find ways to stay in others for free (see "Live in a Castle"), but

THE BIG BUCKET LIST BOOK

Are you of Scottish origin? Or perhaps just fond of the idea of castles, tartans, and titles? For a small sum you too can be a Scottish laird or lady! Check out www.scottishlaird.com. You can buy a square foot of pasture at Dunans Castle, and they will send you an official declaration of your new title. This is an organization working to restore Dunans Castle, so your money goes to a wonderful cause, and of course, you can visit your castle sometime!

what if one day you are struck by the overwhelming need to have a castle of your own?

Castles are largely a European idea. Here in the United States they are simply called mansions, and few are of comparable age to those routinely found in Europe. Westenhanger Castle in Kent, England, was recently on the market for 2.6 million pounds, or about $3.9 million, not too bad considering it has been fully restored from when Henry VIII used it as a place to meet his mistresses. It is also a popular wedding rental venue, so the price included the possible income stream to help the next owner keep up appearances.

A thirty-room French castle in Aix-en-Provence dating from the thirteenth century was listed at $18 million and comes with its own vineyard producing between 150,000 and 200,000 bottles of wine every year. For the really big wallet, Dracula's castle in Romania, known as Bran Castle, is on the market for

$140 million. Built in 1212 and fully restored in the late 1980s, the castle is visited by thousands of paying visitors every year.

If you only have access to somewhat smaller sums, the Castles for Sale website allows hopeful purchasers to list the kind of castle they are seeking. "Looking for a castle in England, Ireland, or Scotland...that can be used as a bed and breakfast," says a gentleman from California. "Willing to consider a fixer-upper" in Austria, says another hopeful future castle owner.

RESOURCES

www.castles-for-sale.com

.... ✳ ....

EPIC EXPERIENCES

Sample Delicious Port in Portugal

Wine tasting is such an ordinary part of life today. Almost every one of the fifty states has a winery and tasting room—yes, even Alaska and Hawaii. And trips to France and Italy are a frequent topic of conversation at dinner parties with your friends. So what is new and different, a challenge? Port, perhaps.

Roxanne Langer, a sommelier, has been to all of the world's wine regions but never passes up a chance for a little fortified wine.

If I could choose any wine region to visit, I would go to Portugal to taste ports where the countryside

Now here is an unusual bucket list item a friend shared with me: "I want my name to be an adjective." Her name is Jeanette, but she goes by JT. How would that work exactly? "Oh, someone might say, 'That is so very JT-esque.' Or, 'Wow, what a JT-ism.'" How would you like your name best used as an adjective? Get to work on that now. You've got a whole year to get yourself and your name declared the new word of the year!

is lovely, the people are nice, the food is fresh and the prices are fabulous! And I wouldn't just stay for a week—the area is worthy of a month's stay, and finding an apartment for a month isn't that difficult. I would stay in either Vila Nova de Gaia, where the port lodges (aging facilities for port) are located, or across the river in Porto, a UNESCO World Heritage Site, which offers a fabulous view of all the different port lodges lining the hillside and shore. Imagine the day trips to the various port houses and regions, stopping for lunch at local village restaurants and getting fresh fish directly from the fishing boats at the wharf for dinner.

Something to dream about as you pour yourself a glass of port after dinner tonight and snack on a few nuts and some blue cheese. You might well book a trip before you finish the glass.

Drink in Gehry's Celebrated Architecture in Spain and France

Frank Gehry, acknowledged as the world's most celebrated living architect, has long been the main reason art lovers flock to Bilbao, Spain. Why? There they can view Gehry's Guggenheim Museum Bilbao, built in 1997.

Now architecture fans and art lovers alike will add Paris to their Gehry-focused trips. The Fondation Louis Vuitton, a museum and cultural center opened in 2014 in the Bois de Boulogne, has quickly been heralded as a masterpiece. Gehry's undulating buildings are instantly recognizable. You could organize your European trips around these two and then head back to the United States to wander up and down the West Coast, stopping first at Seattle's EMP Museum before heading down to Los Angeles to visit his Walt Disney Concert Hall.

www.disneyhall.com

www.empmuseum.org

"The biggest adventure you can ever take
is to live the life of your dreams."
—OPRAH WINFREY

Spend Twelve Months Skiing on the Slopes

You've thought about it late at night while listening to a winter storm, or maybe on a sunny afternoon as you rode up the slopes on a chairlift. "Hmmm…what would it be like to ski year-round? Where would I go… ?" Well, if you're willing to travel a bit, then skiing year-round is possible.

After you have exhausted the winter possibilities at your usual resort, you can head to Canada's Whistler Blackcomb Ski Resort in British Columbia, where you can ski at the very top as late as Canada Day, July 1. Experts only, though, on the top of a glacier where many professional ski teams from around the world practice.

South America is next, with chances to ski in August and September in Chile, Brazil, Argentina, and Peru, among others.

And for the true exotic, try Dubai. Inside of one of the world's biggest malls is Ski Dubai, an indoor snow experience with artificial slopes, jumps, and penguins. Yes, penguins. You don't need to bring all of your equipment. They will rent you not only a board or skis, but also winter clothing. Because who would have that in their closet in Dubai?

Another ski destination where most folks don't own winter clothing is Hawaii. Yes, Hawaii. You will have to bring your equipment and everything with you on this one, as there is no Hawaiian ski industry and no actual resort. However, dedicated skiers can drive a four-wheeler to the top of Mauna Kea and then ski down. This is not for the faint at heart or the short of breath...the air is very thin up there. And when you run out of snow, you don't skid into grass, but lava rock. Ouch. Bear in mind this is a very dangerous pursuit and can cause serious injury.

RESOURCES

www.whistlerblackcomb.com

www.southamericaski.com

www.theplaymania.com/skidubai/welcome

www.hawaiisnowskiclub.com

Take a Trip around the Globe

Is an around-the-world trip on your bucket list too? Are you just waiting for the right moment to pull it off? Sadly, for most of us, that will put it off indefinitely. Publishing entrepreneurs Cindy Bailey and Pierre Giauque thought about it and thought about it, and then they did it.

We have just sold, given away, or trashed 90 percent of our belongings—everything we've accumulated through twelve years of marriage and two kids, now three and nine—in exchange for what we expect will be the experience of a lifetime. Letting go of our home, our school, our community, and saying good-bye to our friends, we plan to travel the world like silly, fun-loving nomads for the next two years.

Although we lived comfortable, secure lives in California, we longed to be free from the burden of our daily routine and obligations, free from constantly chasing the clock. "This is not our lifestyle!" we would say. "This is not us!" So we saved our money, cut expenses, pulled the kids out of school, and went to live the lives intended for us. No use waiting for the kids to grow up. We had to seize the moment now, while we were still energetic and healthy.

We started with the familiar, first traveling to Switzerland, where my husband is from. After three months, we head to Spain for six weeks and then back to the United States to fulfill my husband's dream: to tour as many national parks in the western U.S. and Canada as we can in four months. Finally, from there, we head to Southeast Asia, where our dollar goes far and the culture is immensely rich and rewarding. We will visit Vietnam, Thailand, Laos, Borneo, Bali, and New Zealand. I will work a little along the way to try to push two years into three, and the kids will get an exceptional education. Our business now is to collect experiences, live our adventures, and stuff ourselves with so many rich memories, our perception of time will open and expand exponentially, as it should.

You can find Cindy and her travel blog on Facebook at My Three Little Vagabonds. It might give you the kick you need to leap into your own around-the-world journey, starting now!

RESOURCES

Home Sweet Anywhere: How We Sold Our House, Created a New Life, and Saw the World (Lynne Martin, Sourcebooks, 2014)

http://mylittlevagabonds.com/

Swim from One Continent to Another

Lord Byron did it as a tribute to the myth of Leander and Hero. Caroline Kennedy did it with her daughters, and Bo Derek did it to see if she could. What did they all do? They swam from one continent to another, from Europe to Asia. Sounds tiring, yes, but according to the myth that inspired Byron, Leander did it every night to spend time with his love, Hero.

Are you already an open water swimmer? If not, this is not the sort of athletic challenge you should do as a lark. Best to plunge in and learn to be comfortable swimming in open water somewhere else. Who knows? This could be the reason to undertake a total physical redo and, with the Hellespont Swim as a goal, become the athlete you always hoped to be.

The Dardanelles (formerly known as the Hellespont) is one of the world's busiest waterways, a narrow strait filled with international cargo ships and local commuter ferries, but once a year the traffic is stopped specifically for swimmers to test their endurance. How far is it? Three miles or so. How long does it take? Depends on your swimming ability and speed, of course, and you hope you can do it in the four hours that the ships are held back. In interviews after she finished, Bo Derek told the press that "it was some sort of midlife crisis for sure, probably my third." She trained for a year before attempting the swim and came in sixth in her age group.

Held since 1986, the Hellespont Swim takes place every year on August 30, a date that commemorates a Turkish military victory in their war of independence.

The Swim Hellespont website has the information you need about signing up for a spot. There is a cap on the number of swimmers, so if this is truly a bucket list item for you, start trying to register now.

RESOURCES

www.swimhellespont.com

Embark on an African Safari by Foot

Ever read an article about those brave scientists who go out into the bush to study animals in their natural habitat? The kind of hardy soul who's willing to go again and again to sit quietly near a wild herd until the group grows comfortable. Susan Carson thought that sounded like a challenge and arranged to visit gorillas in their natural environment.

By searching around online I found walkingsafari .com. Now I had been on safari in a Land Rover,

179

which was safe but not very exciting. A walking safari sounded great. My friend and I were sixty-five at the time though, so we thought we should meet the person who'd help us make the arrangements, Robert Brierly, based in Switzerland with his wife and family. He was surprised we were willing to travel so far to organize the trip. No one had ever done that. But our safety was in his hands. He and his family were lovely.

We stayed in Langenthal a few days, visited and planned the trip in detail: what we wanted to see and do, what kind of accommodations we wanted, and how long we were willing to stay. I even asked about visiting a synagogue in eastern Uganda. But what I really wanted to do was hike into the jungle to see the mountain gorillas. I had heard about the adventure, and we were both up for the experience. A real motivator for getting in shape. We picked the dates, based on the best season for travel, and left the rest up to Robert.

And how was it? Susan was thrilled.

It was an amazing experience. More than I expected. We were met at Entebbe by Robert, spent the night at a home and office he owns in Kampala, and took off the following morning. We had a vehicle with a driver for the entire three weeks, and our itinerary was set per our requests. We spent two days doing smaller hikes to see other animals near the Bwindi Impenetrable Forest, where the gorillas were living. That built up the suspense and adventure. But the climax was the day of the big adventure.

Thunder and lightning the night before had me secretly hoping the hike would be canceled. But off we went to meet the Uganda Wildlife Authority, early in the morning. Six people at a time were allowed to go. We were told the rules, no nonsense, and given the option of hiring a porter to help us maneuver the muddy jungle terrain. Five hours of difficult hiking later, under very hot conditions, we were rewarded with a thirty-minute visit with a family of mountain gorillas, silverback and all. What a thrill!

Unfortunately, Susan's guide has passed away, but his wife is carrying on with his company, Nkuringo Safaris. "Regina Brierly will provide the experience of a lifetime," Susan promises.

RESOURCES

www.nkuringosafaris.com

"So the secret is to just say 'yes!' and jump off from here. Then there is no problem. It means to be yourself, always yourself, without sticking to an old self."
—SHUNRYU SUZUKI, FOUNDER OF THE SAN FRANCISCO ZEN CENTER

Jump in with the Big Boys

The idea of swimming with dolphins is on many a bucket list, but what about raising the stakes and swimming with sharks? Yes, it does sound dangerous, but before you go running for safety, consider this: what if they were really big, really slow, really kind sharks that are almost as gentle and friendly toward humans as dolphins? These kinds of sharks do exist: whale sharks. And as the largest living nonmammalian vertebrate, they do not pose a significant danger to humans.

So how can you capture this once-in-a-lifetime experience? Every summer on the Isla Mujeres, off the coast of Cancun, Mexico, whale sharks congregate. And every summer more than a few hearty souls put on fins and snorkels and swim alongside. Scary? Not really, it seems. Steve Broin, the owner of a small hotel there, describes it this way: "The whale sharks are not afraid of us rather diminutive creatures swimming beside them. At times they seem almost humored by our presence."

If the thought of being surrounded by gobs of spring breakers scares you even more than the sharks, don't worry. The Isla Mujeres, the island of women, is not at all like its flashy neighbor, resort and bar-laden Cancun. It's much quieter and calmer. Steve's hotel, Casa Sirena, a small bed-and-breakfast, is the best place to stay. Steve can help you arrange a shark-swimming trip with a licensed captain who has an English-speaking crew member. You can find more information on whale shark tours at the Ceviche Tours website. The season generally runs from the middle of May though the middle of September.

RESOURCES

www.cevichetours.com

www.casasirenamexico.com

Travel Your Own Silk Road

Travel can be organized in so many different ways. For business, to see family, to learn about history or art… Why not fabric as well?

If you're a lover of fashion and furniture, interior design or couture, you could make it a goal to visit the birthplace of your favorite fabric. Silk? Wander the Silk Road anywhere from China and India to the Mediterranean Sea and steep yourself in the rich and sometimes dangerous history of this precious commodity, so critical in driving exploration and trade in centuries past. Jim Thompson Silk in Bangkok is an incredible destination. They are the world's largest maker of handwoven fabrics. The Jim Thompson House and Museum has added a restaurant, and the sales floors have twice yearly markdowns in December and late May.

Velvet more your thing? Luigi Bevilacqua is in the Santa Croce district of Venice. Where did so much of that silk thread end up anyway? Also in Venice you will find the famed Fortuny showroom. To maintain trade secrets, they don't allow factory tours, but the newly renovated gardens are open to the public.

RESOURCES

www.jimthompson.com

www.luigi-bevilacqua.com/en

www.fortuny.com

Have Dinner Up in the Eiffel Tower

The Eiffel Tower is on many a bucket list, but the wait and the crowds are an unexpected downer for many. There are plenty of places in Paris where you can plop down and enjoy a view of the tower in the distance, but what about sitting in an elegant restaurant and looking down on Paris from the Eiffel Tower itself? Not only is the food magnificent at the Jules Verne, but you will jump the line and avoid the crowds by being whisked up in a private elevator that leads to the restaurant on the second level. Four hundred feet above Paris, napkin in your lap and glass of wine at the ready. Paradise found.

Check the website for weekday lunch hours, but you really want the dinnertime experience. Reservations book up far into the future, so the minute you decide you are going to Paris, go to the website and get on the list. The restaurant has been around for years but took a big step up in class and in prices when famed chef Alain Ducasse took over. So be forewarned: this is not an inexpensive undertaking, but rather one that will linger in your memory forever.

RESOURCES

www.lejulesverne-paris.com

Dine Sixty-Five Floors above New York City

The Rainbow Room is back! For those who had a visit to the famed restaurant on top of New York's Rockefeller Plaza on their bucket list but were thwarted by it being closed for several years, get ready meet your goal.

For decades and for several generations, New Yorkers and out-of-town visitors flocked to the restaurant in the sky. And then the building owners closed it. Since reopening in October 2014, the Rainbow Room is mostly available for private events, but it is open for dinner on Monday nights and brunch on Sundays. (Or for a great view without the fabulous dining experience, go to the Observatory Deck at the Top of the Rock.)

While you are at it, if the Tavern on the Green in Central Park was on your longtime list, it also has reopened after several years of hiatus. The reopened restaurant got off to a rocky start in the eyes of New York food critics, but then famed chef Jeremiah Tower came out of retirement to give it a boost. Stop in and see if that worked.

RESOURCES

www.rainbowroom.com

www.topoftherock.com

www.tavernonthegreen.com

Travel with Your Favorite Baseball Team

Devoted to your hometown team? Catch a home game at the local stadium as often as possible? What about taking it up a notch and traveling with the team? Okay, maybe not on the same bus, but perhaps staying in the same hotel. Debbie Ammerman tells us how.

*I love to visit U.S. cities, and Rex loves baseball…
so we are aiming to see the SF Giants play in as
many different cities as we can. It's a lot more than
just going to the game. It's the experience of visiting
another baseball park, the people, and their city.*

*It's easy to sit in AT&T Park where you are with
42,000 people wearing the same jersey, but when
you meet your team's fans in another city you are
coconspirators. It's fun walking into another team's
stadium and showing your colors. There is a camara-
derie that takes place with your fellow fans. It starts
when you board your plane. Then you run into them
in bars, you see them on subways, you see them on
the street. There is a kinship. You make eye contact,
you immediately bond.*

*We went to New York to see the SF Giants
play first the Yankees and then the Mets, two teams
and two stadiums in one city. I boarded my subway*

187

train, and virtually everyone in that compartment had a Giants uniform on. It's so much fun. There is a San Francisco sports bar in New York City called Finnerty's, and when you walk in, it's like being in a bar in San Francisco with Giants fans.

Lots of fans stay at the same hotel as the team. It's cool because you are staying with the team while attending the game. In San Diego we stayed at the Omni, and the players, broadcasters, and their families were there with us. You run into the players getting coffee, eating dinner, or riding the elevator. No one makes a big deal of it. Fans respect the players' privacy, and it makes the experience so enjoyable.

Is that it? Are Rex and Debbie done with their baseball journeys? Of course not. "Next is Wrigley Field to see the iconic Chicago Cubs and their stadium. Can't wait to check out the city and support our team!"

An even bigger bucket-list goal is to visit as many of the major league ballparks around the country as possible—or perhaps all. That is what television reporter Mike Luery did with his son, Matt. Not in one summer though. It took sixteen years to hit every park on the list. Mike wrote about the experience in his book *Baseball Between Us*.

Baseball is a game of numbers. Batting averages, runs batted in, and winning percentages are the currency of America's national pastime. But there is also great value in being in the ballpark, especially with someone you love. When my son, Matt, was just five, I discovered that he savored the smell of Cracker Jack and the taste of a hot dog smothered in mustard as much as I do. I knew we had to hit the road for the ultimate baseball experience.

Together, we traveled 43,000 miles over sixteen years to attend baseball games in thirty-two different venues, from Fenway Park in Boston to Dodger Stadium in Los Angeles. It was the ultimate father-son bonding experience born from a bucket list to visit every major league park in North America.

Traveling by train, plane, and automobile we fought over food, music, and bedtime, but by the time the journey ended, Matt was twenty-one—and we could celebrate our accomplishment by drinking beers together at the ballpark. For me, it was the ultimate parenting experience, and I know my son loved it too because he told me, "Dad, we will always have baseball between us."

RESOURCES

www.baseballbetweenus.com

Own a Tiny House Just for You

Worn down by everything in your life? Might be time to go small. Build a tiny house, drive a smallish car, give away much of the stuff that clutters your house. As we move through life, the things we own often tie us in place, working a job we don't like and living in an area that doesn't make our spirits soar. If you didn't have those things, that big house, the large gas bill, would you be able to do more of the things that you have written down as life goals?

The current small-house movement was sparked by architect Susan Susanka and her 1998 book *The Not So Big House*. Tiny house proponent Jay Shafer built his first Tumbleweed house on a truck bed in 1999, and the small and tiny spark grew from there.

Could you live in a house that was just 120 square feet? Maybe you could. Pare down your possessions and give it a try. Tiny houses are just that, tiny. Not-so-big houses come in a far greater range of sizes and are an easier step down from our traditional house size. Maybe you will start small and then graduate to tiny.

RESOURCES

www.notsobighouse.com

www.fourlightshouses.com

Let's Go Racing: Be Part of a Car Race

Not everyone is a NASCAR fan. Those oval tracks look tedious. Maybe it's time to take up road racing. If you no longer need to worry about setting a good example for the kids, why not stomp on the gas pedal and let it fly around a road-racing track, hairpin turns and all? Racing doesn't have to be the billionaires' sport of Formula One. It can be as simple as taking your everyday car out on a track for a timed trial.

Ordinary America races with the SCCA, the Sports Car Club of America. Founded in 1944, the club has 115 regions around the country, so no doubt one is near you. In addition to actual driving, you can get your racing thrills by volunteering with the SCCA for events. You could work as an on-course flagger, an official, a timer, or a scorer. Don't worry, they don't expect

The least attractive picture ever taken of me was for my SCCA racing license. In the photo I looked like I'd just escaped from prison, hair disheveled and a startled expression on my pasty face. But hey, it was a racing license. How cool is that? In fact, learning to drive a race car is the opposite of scary—it is a feeling of great safety as you strap into the H belt (far more secure than the tiny straps that hold us in place in our regular cars), pull on a helmet, and drive out onto a course in a car with a roll cage. Makes everyday freeway driving feel very threatening by comparison!

volunteers to show up knowing how to do these tasks, but they're easy to learn.

If you really do want to drive fast, what then? Try solo events, autocross competitions that are all about timing and individual driving skill on a traffic-cone course. Or vintage racing, which is an elegant undertaking by old cars in which the drivers make it a point not to hit one other. After all, who wants a ding in their old Jag? Wheel-to-wheel racing pits you against a field of other cars on a track, and you'll need to be assertive.

A full description of all of the different types of racing available through the SCCA can be found at www.goaheadtakethewheel.com.

Surf the Best Waves in Europe

Americans can surf in Hawaii, in Mexico, on the California coast, and along the shores of Long Island. If you are a surfer, why not make it a goal to pack your board and head overseas? Finish with summer surfing on the beaches here and then head for the autumn swells on the Atlantic coast. Northern France, Portugal, and even Wales have established surfing communities. The Azores, nine islands in the

Atlantic a thousand or so miles from Lisbon, have been referred to by one surfing blog as the "Atlantic Hawaii." At least one professional surfing event has been held there, so the Azores are beginning to be discovered by the rest of the surfing community.

Why not find out what the world's waves have to offer you? Bragging rights, if nothing else.

.... ✳ ....

GLAMOROUS GOALS
AND GETAWAYS

Snuggle Up in an Ice Hotel

Ice hotels. What an astonishing idea—to build a new structure every year, furnish and staff it fully, welcome guests for a few short months, and then watch all of your hard work melt slowly away... So each year, each crop of guests is exposed to a true work of unique art and architecture that will disappear and be resurrected slightly differently the next year.

Where can you find ice hotels? In very cold places like Sweden, Iceland, and Canada. The original is Icehotel in Jukkasjärvi, Sweden. First opened in 1990 and rebuilt every year since, it can accommodate around a hundred guests. In Quebec you will find

Hôtel de Glace, the first North American ice hotel. In Finland you can stay in a castle made from ice, Snow Castle, in Kemi. For twenty years the castle has been built on the Gulf of Bothnia, and it includes a public restaurant in case you don't want to spend the whole night in an icy room.

You can also try building an icehouse of your own. The Urban Gardens website has a charming story about some New Zealanders who built their own backyard igloo out of colorful ice blocks made from hundreds of empty milk cartons. This could be a project that will keep you busy all winter long!

RESOURCES

www.icehotel.com

www.hoteldeglace-canada.com

www.visitkemi.fi/en/snowcastle

www.urbangardensweb.com/?s=igloo

"The purpose of life is to live it, to taste experience to the utmost, to reach out eagerly and without fear for the newer and richer experience."
—ELEANOR ROOSEVELT

Get Done Up and Be a Star in Photos

Ever looked with envy at a friend's new Facebook photo? Just too, too perfect and glamorous. While yours shows you in an old sweatshirt, hugging your dog. Chances are your friend had a little work done before her photo was taken. No, not actual plastic surgery. Just a professional makeup job. Sure it is a splurge, but don't you deserve it every once in a while?

When you're getting ready for the big event, be it a wedding, a big social event, or a romantic evening for two, it is best to spend the money and have your makeup done twice. Once to test it out and see if you like what they do, and the second time for the actual event. Imagine your dismay if, after an hour or so in front of the mirror just before your event is to start, you look up and gasp at the sight of an overly done face.

You can always place yourself in the hands of the makeup artists in department stores who do it for free, with the understanding that when they are done you may be so delighted that you'll buy many of the products they used on you. So why not step up your glamour game every so often and bask in the compliments.

Have a Dish at a Restaurant Named after You

It is human to want the world to know our names, who we are. Some folks like to see their name emblazoned on the side of a building, attached to a charity, or used as the basis for a business. Not all of us want to be so grand, but wouldn't it be fun to open the menu at a favorite restaurant and find a sandwich named after ourselves?

How? Well, best if it is a fairly casual place you frequent, and the owners or managers are accustomed to you stopping in regularly. The sort of place where they smile and nod as you come in, already sensing just what you might order… Do you have a favorite dish? Or perhaps you ask for a customized version of something already on the menu? Then speak up and ask that it be named after you. Offer to make a donation to the owner's favorite charity in exchange for a shout-out on the menu. Who knows? They may go for it, and you'll return the favor by coming in even more than you did before!

Celebrate Mardi Gras without the Crowds

How can you attend Mardi Gras in New Orleans and not have to stand in a packed and noisy crowd of strangers on a smelly street? Well, you could ride on a float and look out at the crowds from your coveted place on the ride. Maybe you've always dreamed of that, but you understand that the krewes are all old-guard New Orleans folks who won't let anyone else play. Sometimes yes, sometimes no…

"You can buy your way in," says event planner Ingrid Lundquist. Her husband, Tom LaMair, answered a "Want to ride on a float?" ad in *Gourmet* magazine years ago and surprised her with the experience. *Gourmet* magazine is long gone but the opportunities have only increased. Among the krewes that will sell you an annual membership that includes riding on the float are the Krewe of Pygmalion, the Krewe of Napoleon, and the Krewe of Pontchartrain. Prices range from $275 for the Krewe of Napoleon to more than $1,000 for the deluxe membership in the Krewe of Pygmalion.

All of the various memberships include not only a spot on the float but also an after-party. Be prepared…this is not a quick jaunt around the block. These are three- to four-hour parades, and yes, some of the floats have bathrooms!

The Krewe of Pygmalion's website has all the information you need to join and ride in next year's parade.

Looking for a Mardi Gras and Carnival experience out of the country but not ready to try the scene in Brazil? Mexico's biggest and best Mardi Gras celebration takes place in La Paz, on the Baja Peninsula.

RESOURCES

www.kreweofpygmalion.org

www.bajapiratesoflapaz.com

Up, Up, and Away! Ride in an Old-Fashioned Airplane

Another day, another plane ride. Air travel is so humdrum nowadays, not in the least bit exciting or sexy. But what if you could ride in a glider? A seaplane? An open-cockpit aircraft? Stephanie Taylor leads a life filled with excitement of the art variety—installing large sculptures and murals that she designs—but she'd longed to ride in an old-fashioned airplane. And so she did.

The pilot turns a sleek wooden propeller by hand, as if the plane is going to fly by a tensioned rubber band. The single engine of the 1943 Stearman catches with a throaty roar. Like aviation pioneers, I'd always wanted to fly in such a tiny, vulnerable craft, mere canvas stretched over wooden frame, one bright yellow wing over the other, cockpit open to the wind, the sound, the sun.

Flying over rice fields, we bank hard. Wings dip and down we go, low, very low, leveling off just feet from the ground. Each little green blade of new growth sticks up through shallow water, almost tickling the bottom of the plane. Pulling hard on the stick, we reach for the sky. And down we go, diving. In the banked turn, gravity has no pull, no g-force, just steeply angled to 45 degrees, looking straight to earth, graceful and eerily silent within my leather helmet.

Outside the protection of the windshield, my hand hits a hurricane-force 100 mph slipstream that could rip my watch right off my wrist. I look down at the stick between my legs that looks most like a baseball bat and at my feet resting on the metal floor, safely away from the brakes. "Don't put your feet on those pedals," the pilot warns. "Whatever you do, don't touch them." The implications are obvious.

Would she do it again? "Yes, I'd do it again. The pilot asked if I wanted to take the controls, and I would have but didn't want to miss all the sensations at that moment. So perhaps if I do it again, I'd accept that challenge."

You can fly over Florida in a biplane out of the Orlando Executive airport. In Ohio you can find Goodfolk and O'Tymes Biplane Rides operating out of Dayton, Cincinnati, and Columbus.

RESOURCES

www.floridabiplanes.com

www.gobiplanerides.com

Shop the Best Flea Markets

"Oh this? I found it at the Paris flea market and had it shipped back..." Could there be a more casually sophisticated response to a guest's question about your antique chair? The Paris flea market, London's Portobello Market, the bazaar in Istanbul... Surround yourself with large treasures from your travels.

The grande dame of the Paris flea markets (there are several) is Clignancourt, on the edge of the Eighteenth Arrondissement. You could spend days and days perusing all of the various stalls there. A good source of information is Dixon Long and Marjorie

"Passport, please." Although there is a widely held rumor that only around 10 percent of Americans have passports, the true number is closer to 42 percent, according to William Chalmers, author of the book *America's Vacation Deficit Disorder*. Are you among them? If not, gather up your birth certificate and get over to the post office. Mexico and Canada are both off limits to U.S. citizens without valid passports, and the days when we could all cross back and forth with little or no identification are long gone. So make sure that you could join a friend on a whim at a moment's notice, whether you're visiting one of our neighbors north or south or off on a bigger trip across the pond.

Williams's book *Markets of Paris*. The book also highlights many other smaller markets, like the Saint-Paul Antiques Village in the Marias. Read Marjorie's blog for more inside shopping tips.

What to do once you found the perfect couch for your house in Houston? However can you get it home? Call Hedley's Humpers. A large company devoted to helping with this problem, they maintain offices at the major flea markets and will help you ship directly from there. You can also find information on all of the major antique fairs in the UK and Europe on their website, with info on the fairs where they will have their shipping services available.

RESOURCES

www.marjorierwilliams.com

www.hedleyshumpers.com

Markets of Paris, 2nd Edition: Food, Antiques, Crafts, Books, and More. Dixon Long and Marjorie R. Williams, Little Bookroom, 2012)

Do What Scares You

Really, what does scare you the most? Whatever it is, getting over your fear is a worthy bucket-list item to achieve. It is high time, don't you think?

Does public speaking scare you? No problem. Join a speaking group like Toastmasters International. There is a chapter near you. Afraid to express your opinion? Sit down and write a letter to the editor every week about something in the news. You might not mail them at first, but eventually you will work up the nerve to hit Send. Terrified of heights? Start by walking up the indoor steps of a very tall building and work up to looking out the window once you are at the top. The exercise will do you good. Afraid to fly? There are many programs out there to help you overcome that, and some are sponsored by the airline industry! Body issues? Take up dancing and get out there and move. Shake it.

Think how exciting and full of new adventures this next phase in your life could be if you just got past the fears that are holding you back!

RESOURCES

www.toastmasters.org

Glam It Up!

Shake the wrinkles out of your gown, dust off the tuxedo, and head out the door. What's that you say? There aren't any fancy occasions on your calendar? Why let that hold you back? No reason to pout when you can easily create your own glamorous lifestyle by dressing up whenever the whim strikes and heading out on the town.

No need to feel foolish. No one will suspect that you aren't on your way to somewhere fabulous or on your way back from someplace spectacular. Act as though you always dress this way. Don't blush or giggle. Or go ahead and blush and giggle if that adds to the occasion!

The best places to go in black tie if you haven't really been out to a black tie event are to an all-night diner after midnight (Have a hot turkey sandwich and complain loudly about how the food is always so skimpy at the gala…) or a bar after eleven or so. Imagine how you will feel perched on a bar stool while your long dress puddles around you on the floor, or when you slip your hand inside your tuxedo to reach for your wallet while settling the tab. Life is a banquet indeed, and most poor suckers are starving. Isn't that what Auntie Mame said so famously? So don't feel starved for invitations. Head out on the town on your own.

> "One does not discover new lands without consenting to lose sight of the shore for a very long time."
> **—ANDRE GIDE**

Shhhhh! No Talking: Go on a Silent Retreat

Our world is a noisy one. From your cell-phone-gabbing seatmate on the commuter train to the endless soundtrack that follows us through every retail store and the constant blare of horns and screech of brakes, isn't it enough to make you want to just walk away and seek a quiet spot to refocus?

You can in any one of a number of silent retreat spots around the country. You can create your own silent retreat for free, of course, by simply shutting off your phone, radio, and television, and vowing to focus instead on your own breathing for an hour, an afternoon, or a weekend. If you would like to seek silence in the company of others, try some of these places. Some are totally silent, while others will give you the space to create your own retreat into quietness.

Gonzaga Eastern Point Retreat House, Gloucester, Massachusetts—run by the Jesuits. (www.easternpoint.org)

Green Gulch Farm, Muir Beach, California—an offshoot of the San Francisco Zen Center, Green Gulch offers a wide variety of retreats and classes. (www.sfzc.org/ggf/default.asp)

Breitenbush Hot Springs, Detroit, Oregon—they offer quiet weekends. (www.breitenbush.com)

Esalen, Big Sur, California—one of the granddaddies of the New Age movement, Esalen Institute on the central California coast is well known for not only its cliffside hot tub, but also its focus on spiritual growth. (www.esalen.org)

Get a Producer Credit in a Documentary

In the movie business, where your name appears in the credits is of tremendous importance. For instance, a recent opportunity on Kickstarter from the folks at the Henry Miller Library in Big Sur, California, offered the "executive producer" credit to anyone who donated $5,000 to the documentary they were putting together about Miller's days in Paris. For $2,500 you could be listed as an "associate producer." All you would have to do is write a check.

And other than the chance to tell your friends you've helped fund an art-house documentary, what else do you get? Perhaps the chance to come to Sundance or another film fest to watch the fruits of your funding.

But if you don't have a friend who is working on a documentary, how can you find these kinds of opportunities? Kickstarter is full of them. Recent opportunities to be listed as a producer for several grand include a documentary about cigar-box guitars (they would also come to your house and put on a show), a documentary examining the harsh lives of children who work in gold mining fields, or a film on the global obsession with painted fingernails. Really.

RESOURCES

www.kickstarter.com

Dress to the Nines: Rent the Runway and Wear Couture Fashion

Is wearing couture clothing on your bucket list? Many women fantasize about someday sashaying into a big public event sheathed in an expensive designer dress. Gucci. Dior. Badgley Mischka. Alexander McQueen. Designer consignment stores around the country are a good place to look if you want couture items hanging in your closet, but what if all you really want is that one-night experience? Well, you really can rent the runway.

Rent the Runway is an online clothing rental company with a fairly simple business model. You scroll around the site looking at the dresses, order what you want, and it arrives on your doorstep. You wear it to great acclaim, return it in the package they provided, and poof, the dress disappears. You wore it, you loved it, and you didn't have to take out a bank loan for the experience.

"Over the last few years, friends have been getting married at an insane pace," says Lisa Kapasi, "and lately the events have all been black tie. My husband has a tux, but I can't stock my closet with full-length formals. I used Rent the Runway and had a Carolina Herrera dress delivered to our hotel, and when I took the dress out of the box I was immediately in love. I've seen celebrities walk the red carpet in this dress! I felt beautiful, stunning, and confident."

Recent examples are a Carolina Herrera ball gown that retails for $3,590 but rents for $475; a $3,200 Blumarine cocktail dress that you can wear for $350; or a $500 ML Monique Lhuillier dress that rents for $95. There are prices that will fit all budgets. And don't worry about whether your order will fit. They routinely send the dress in two different sizes so that you are assured one will do the trick.

RESOURCES

www.renttherunway.com

Say Yes to Your Next Opportunity!

Here's a great bucket list vow—say yes to some unexpected opportunity. Say yes the next time a friend asks you to go somewhere. Say yes the next time the waiter asks if you want dessert. Say yes the next time a sibling wants to come and stay.

If you're feeling in a rut and don't seem to have any choices to say yes to, you can quickly jolt yourself out of an old established routine by asking someone to make a choice for you. Ask the waiter what they'd have for dinner and then try it. Ask a friend what movie you should see. Ask the bookstore employee (yes, go to an independent bookstore!) what they most enjoyed reading. Ask the bartender to make you something unusual and surprising that's not on the menu. Ask your children what they think you should do this coming weekend.

We all spend so much time saying "no" to things. Often it is the first thought that comes to mind. So why not try being a person with a default switch set to "yes" and see where it might take you next!

·········· ✸ ··········

AFTERWORD

N ow that you've gotten to the end of the book, hopefully you've found many ideas and experiences that appeal to you. But how do you put them into action and make sure you actually achieve them? Follow these two surprisingly simple rules:

1. Enlist Your Friends and Family

   Yep, bucket lists don't have to be individual to each of us. Instead, involve your friends and family. Tell everyone what you hope to accomplish, and ask them to join in. Encourage them to join you on special trips, with personal goals, or in creating lasting change in your life. Being part of a group will help keep you on target to achieve your goals—and you'll enjoy the experience more when sharing it with those you love.

Picture this—you want to write a play. Rather than do all of this in secret and have to shoulder all the work, why not tell your friends and family and enlist them to help with the process by reciting dialog or acting out a rough part? They can even give you constructive feedback on your project, so you don't have to wonder for months or maybe years whether you created a worthy project. Setting goals and doing anything creative can feel like a lonely individual process, but it doesn't have to be. Any kind of goal or dream can be achieved more quickly if you are out in the open about it. Everyone in your life wants to see you succeed and be happy, so let them help you.

Travel goals are the same, a chance to let others in on what you are longing to do. Tell everyone what you have in mind, and you might begin to hear things like this:

"Paris? My cousin has an apartment there. I'll ask if you can use it."

"An ice hotel? I've always wanted to go to one. Let's share a room!"

"A pilgrimage down Route 66? Let's take my old Ford Mustang!"

Suddenly what started as a dream seems a lot more realistic.

2. Write Down Your Goals

Goal setting is not something that came naturally to me. After bumping into Mark Victor Hansen, the coauthor of the *Chicken Soup for the Soul* inspirational book series on many occasions and listening to his motivational speeches, I finally sat down and did as he said. I wrote out 101 goals in purple ink.

"Purple is the highest color," he had said before repeating one of his mantras. "Don't just think it, ink it!" Fifteen years later, I have achieved a healthy number of those original 101 goals, some of which were quite lofty (Raise Wise Sons) and some of which were pretty selfish (Wear More Cashmere). I still need to Brush Up My Latin, but hey, you have to keep something out there to reach for.

Writing out your goals is a fun exercise, but to really get motivated, make it an event. Don't just tap them into your iPad or phone. Sit down with some nice stationery and a quality pen. Pour a little wine, or sit in a window with a beckoning view. Perhaps light a scented candle if you have one nearby.

Create some atmosphere, and then let your mind and imagination run wild. Write down crazy things too—you are just warming up and they don't have to be on your actual bucket list. Most of all, write as if money, time, space, physics, and time are no object. With the right mindset, when you set out to make these things happen, the ordinary obstacles just might fall away.

In closing, remember the three steps to insider status and the chance for a once-in-a-lifetime opportunity:

1. Volunteer—Volunteering at a museum you love or for a cause that animates you will bring you into contact with like-minded people who share your interests and might well have the knowledge or contacts or ideas to help you achieve your goals.

2. Join support groups—Simply by sending in the smallest amount to belong to a "friends of" organization, you will begin to receive the newsletter and be kept apprised of the activities and opportunities

that others will not know about. Behind-the-scenes tours, special events inside a building you long to know better, or the chance to travel with others who share your interest will all come your way for a modest investment.

3. Charity auction items—A trip to fashion week in Paris? An exotic dinner party inside a zoo? The chance to fly in a vintage plane? The chance to have your name used as a character in a book by one of your favorite authors? These kinds of unusual opportunities are routinely made available at charity auctions. Attend these events on a regular basis and you will have the chance to lead a far more interesting life, should you have the wallet and bank account to back it up.

So, which of the things in this book are on my own personal bucket list? Well, here are a few goals I have set for myself in the coming years:

Commission an opera from a major composer, based on a well-known literary work, to be performed by a major opera company.

Visit the Jim Thompson House in Bangkok and dine on the patio.

Perfect the recipe for boeuf bourguignon (the real one, not the Julia Child shortcut!).

Write a book on Paris while living in Paris and give an author talk at Shakespeare and Company.

Learn more Latin.

Attend a function at the White House.

Explore Yellowstone National Park through all five different entrances (only two left to go!).

Feel free to send me an email at basyesander@yahoo.com. Tell me what's on your list and ask whether I've gotten anywhere close to my dreams. Enjoy!

INDEX

---- ✳ ----

ABOUT THE AUTHOR

 Gin Sander is the author of several lifestyle books, including *The Martini Diet* and *Wear More Cashmere.* She divides her time between a house in California's Sierra foothills and a cottage at Lake Tahoe, but is hardly ever home. You might bump into her in line at the airport someday.